| 汉英对照 |

中国关键词

出彩河南篇

Henan Province

KEYWORDS TO UNDERSTAND CHINA

权威解读当代中国

中国外文出版发行事业局
当代中国与世界研究院
中国翻译研究院
中共河南省委外事工作委员会办公室

新世界出版社
NEW WORLD PRESS

First Edition 2024

Compiled by
China International Communications Group
Academy of Contemporary China and World Studies
China Academy of Translation
Office of the Foreign Affairs Commission of the Henan Provincial Committee of the Communist Party of China

Translated by
Xiang Na

English text edited by
Salil Bissessur, Han Qingyue, and Song Jinying

Cover designed by
Wei Fangfang and He Yuting

ISBN 978-7-5104-7774-4

Published by
NEW WORLD PRESS
24 Baiwanzhuang Street, Beijing 100037, China

Distributed by
NEW WORLD PRESS
24 Baiwanzhuang Street, Beijing 100037, China
Tel: 86-10-68995968
Fax: 86-10-68998705
Website: www.nwp.com.cn
E-mail: nwpcd@sina.com

Printed in the People's Republic of China

Keywords to Understand China: Henan Province

Editorial Committee

前　言

距今 25 亿年前，位于当今中国河南省中部的嵩山从苍茫浩瀚的大海中古陆崛起，横空出世，成为欧亚大陆板块中最先露出海平面的陆地。岁月荏苒，沧海桑田，大自然的鬼斧神工造就了今日雄浑壮丽的中原。黄河、淮河、长江、海河等中国最重要的大川从这里流过，冲积沃野，滋养两岸，孕育了中华民族。以河南为腹地的中原大地如木之根本、水之渊源，成为华夏儿女的心灵故乡和精神家园。

自公元前 21 世纪起，夏、商、周王朝在中原地区连续建都，被尊为“中央王朝”“中央之国”，最早的“中国”蹒跚起步，20 多个朝代、200 多个皇帝在此执掌江山社稷 3000 多年。行走河南，可以一览中华文明从孕育到形成的完整过程，可以读懂中华民族怎样筚路蓝缕创造了 5000 多年生生不息的中华文明。

古往今来，这片古老厚重的土地见证了中华民族历经磨难而坚韧不拔的顽强斗志，造就了以爱国主义为核心的创造精神、奋斗精神、团结精神、梦想精神，镌刻着中华民族从站起来、富起来到强起来的壮阔历程和翻天覆地的变化。

无论是历史的厚重灿烂，还是当今的日新月异，河南都是中国最具代表性的一个缩影。读懂河南，才能理解今日中国何以中国，中华文化何以博大精深、延绵不断；行走河南，方能感受更加出彩的中原，感知可信、可爱、可敬的中国。

为讲好河南故事，增进外国受众对河南的了解，“中国关键词”多语对外传播平台组织策划了《中国关键词：出彩河南篇》。本篇按照史话河南、走进河南、展望河南的编写逻辑，选取 60 个关键词进行简明扼要的介绍和解读。我们深知，仅用几十个关键词，很难全景式展现河南的历史、当下与未来。我们的全部努力在于，为读者提供一把感知、认识、读懂河南的钥匙。本书为中外对照版，由于能力及时间所限，在中文词条遴选编写时，难免挂一漏万。同时，为使译文更符合目标语读者的阅读习惯，我们对翻译表达进行了创新探索，旨在提升读者的阅读体验。

“中国关键词”多语对外传播平台是中国外文出版发行事业局、当代中国与世界研究院、中国翻译研究院联合实施的国家对外话语创新重点项目，通过平面、网络和移动社交平台等多媒体、多渠道、多语种、多形态及时持续对外发布，旨在以外国受众易于阅读和理解的方式，向世界介绍新时代的中国。

讲故事需要关键词，讲好中国故事需要中国关键词。让我们用“中国关键词”读懂中国、沟通世界。

Introduction

About 2.5 billion years ago, the Songshan Mountain, which is located in central Henan Province today, rose from the bottom of the boundless ocean and became the first part of the Eurasian continent to emerge above the sea. Through the ages, enormous changes have taken place on earth, and the magic hands of mother nature have crafted the vast Central Plains, where four major rivers – Yellow, Huaihe, Yangtze, and Haihe – or their tributaries have irrigated the fertile lands and nourished the Chinese nation. This makes the Central Plains in the middle and lower reaches of the Yellow River, with Henan Province in the center, a cultural home and an anchor of the souls of the Chinese people, like the root of a giant tree and the fountainhead of a great river.

Starting from the 21st century BC, the Xia, the Shang, and the Zhou dynasties had built their capitals in the Central Plains in succession. Generally known as the "central dynasties" or "central states," they were the initial form of what we know as China today. From then on, more than 200 emperors of over 20 dynasties had ruled the country from here for more than 3,000 years. A journey through Henan will take you through the whole history of the Chinese civilization – how it was created and has been sustained by the Chinese nation over more than 5,000 years.

Through the long river of history, the Central Plains

have witnessed how the indomitable Chinese nation has survived numerous tribulations and fostered its creativity, fighting spirit, solidarity, and ambition with deep patriotism at the core. This land recorded the nation's tremendous transformation from standing up and growing prosperous to becoming strong.

Henan Province is a perfect epitome of China, both for its rich history and rapid development today. Understanding Henan will help one understand how China has become what it is today and how the Chinese culture has continued uninterrupted and become so extensive. Traveling in Henan will enable one to see the splendid Central Plains, an important window into the credible, appealing, and respectable China.

To offer a straightforward narrative of Henan and help global readers learn more about the province, the "China Keywords" multilingual platform has produced this booklet – *Keywords to Understand China: Henan Province*, presenting the past, the present, and the prospects of Henan with 60 keyword entries. We are aware that this is far from enough to cover the whole picture and that much more may be desired, so this book will serve as a key to open the gate to the treasure house of Henan and spark the readers' interest in further exploration.

Due to the scope of this work and its tight schedule, there may be oversights or inaccuracies in our selection of entries. To make the English version accessible to an international audience, the English editors made alterations where they thought necessary, which might lead to inconsistencies between the Chinese and English texts.

The "China Keywords" platform is a major national project implemented by the China International Communications Group, the Academy of Contemporary China and World Studies, and the China Academy of Translation to offer an authoritative guide to understanding contemporary China in the new era. This multilingual platform can be accessed online and via mobile social media.

Keywords are at the heart of any story. "China Keywords" are at the heart of the story of China. We hope that the project will help build a bridge of understanding between China and the rest of the world.

Contents
目 录

史话河南篇

“最早的中国”
China in the Initial Form 002

伏羲
Fuxi 006

炎黄二帝
Yandi and Huangdi 010

大禹治水
Da Yu Harnessing the Floods 014

中华姓氏之源
Origins of Chinese Surnames 018

仰韶文化
Yangshao Culture 020

河洛文化
Heluo Culture 024

木兰文化
Hua Mulan 026

愚公移山
The Old Man Yu Gong Moving the Mountains 030

二十四节气
The Twenty-Four Solar Terms 034

河图洛书
Hetu and *Luoshu* 038

《说文解字》
Shuo Wen Jie Zi 042

《易经》
Yi Jing 046

儒释道
Confucianism, Buddhism, and Daoism 050

老子
Lao Zi 056

庄子
Zhuang Zi 060

张仲景
Zhang Zhongjing 062

玄奘
Xuanzang 066

杜甫
Du Fu 070

得中原者得天下
He Who Controls the Central Plains Will Control the Whole Country 072

走进河南篇

II

华夏古都
The Ancient Capital Cities 078

安阳殷墟
Yin Xu in Anyang 082

登封“天地之中”历史建筑群
Historic Monuments of Dengfeng in “The Center of Heaven and Earth” 086

“中华第一龙”
No. 1 Dragon in China 090

洛阳龙门石窟
Longmen Grottoes in Luoyang 094

洛阳白马寺
Baima Temple in Luoyang 098

洛阳牡丹甲天下
Luoyang Peony, Queen of Flowers 102

大运河河南段
Henan Sections of the Grand Canal 106

丝绸之路河南段崤函古道
Xiaohan Ancient Path of the Silk Road 110

云台山世界地质公园
Yuntaishan Global Geopark 114

少林功夫
Shaolin *Kung Fu* 118

太极拳
Taijiquan 122

《清明上河图》
Qing Ming Shang He Tu 126

商丘火神台庙会
Huoshentai Temple Fair in Shangqiu 130

重阳节
Chongyang Festival 134

豫剧
Yuju Opera 136

《唐宫夜宴》
Night Banquet in the Tang Dynasty Palace 138

钧瓷 · 汝瓷
Jun Porcelain and Ru Porcelain 142

四大怀药
Four Renowned Huai Medicines 146

信阳毛尖
Xinyang Maojian Tea 150

河南烩面
Henan Stewed Noodles 154

道口烧鸡
Daokou Red-Cooked Chicken 158

红旗渠
Hongqi Canal 160

焦裕禄
Jiao Yulu 164

展望河南篇

III

黄河流域生态保护和高质量发展
Ecological Protection and High-Quality Development of the Yellow River Basin 170

“打好四张牌”
Four Strong Cards for Henan's Development 174

“两个确保”
Two Goals for Mid-21st Century Henan 180

“十大战略”
Ten Strategies 184

郑洛新国家自主创新示范区
Zhengzhou-Luoyang-Xinxiang National Innovation Demonstration Zone 190

南水北调中线工程
Middle Route of the South-to-North Water Diversion Project........194

乡村振兴
Rural Revitalization........198

“中原农谷”
Central Plains Agricultural Valley........202

国人厨房
Kitchen of China........206

中原城市群
Central Plains City Cluster........210

郑州航空港经济综合实验区
Zhengzhou Airport Economy Zone........214

中国（河南）自由贸易试验区
China (Henan) Pilot Free Trade Zone........218

四路协同
Four-Route Silk Road........222

建设四大国家文化公园
Four National Cultural Parks........228

行走河南 · 读懂中国
Walking Through Henan, Understanding China........232

“老家河南”
Sweet Home Henan........236

史话河南篇

I

“最早的中国”

中华文明起源于黄河流域，位于其中下游、以河南为中心的中原地区，土地肥沃、气候宜人，上古时期的华夏先民以部落的形式在这里繁衍生息。

中华民族的人文始祖之一黄帝在河南新郑诞生、创业、建都，代表了华夏文明的最初自觉，标志着“中国”观念的萌芽。出现于公元前14世纪的殷商后期的“甲骨文”被认为是“汉字”的第一种形式。距今大约3800—3500年的二里头遗址是迄今所知中国最早的广域王权国家的都城，是探索中国早期文明和国家起源、夏文化、夏商王朝纪年及其分界

China in the Initial Form

The Chinese civilization originated in the Yellow River basin. The Central Plains, located in the middle and lower reaches of the Yellow River with Henan in the center, had nurtured and sustained the tribes of the Huaxia – an ancient appellation of the Han people, which is also used to call the Chinese nation or China – with fertile lands and a pleasant climate in remote antiquity.

Huangdi, or the Yellow Emperor, a legendary progenitor of the Chinese nation, was said to be born in Xinzheng of Henan Province today. Later he became a capable tribal leader and built the capital here. That was the earliest formation of the Huaxia, or Chinese, civilization, giving rise to the initial notion of "Zhongguo" (literally "central state"), the Chinese name of "China." The oracle-bone inscriptions that appeared in the 14th century BC, during the Shang Dynasty (1600-1046 BC) are regarded as the first form of Chinese characters. The Erlitou site, dating back 3,500-3,800 years, was the capital of the earliest state discovered so far in Chinese history where the kings exercised rule over a large region. It is of vital importance for tracing the origin and early-stage civilization of China, determining the chronicles of and the demarcation between the Xia (c. 2070-1600 BC) and the Shang dynasties, and studying the Xia culture. As the earliest core culture in

的关键性遗址。二里头文化是中国乃至东亚地区最早的“核心文化”，所代表的青铜时代产生了私有制和阶级的萌芽，确立了国家形态，开启了王朝时代，并且形成了“择中建国”等政治理念，从而形成了政治上“最早的中国”，标志着中国历史进入文明时代。后续王朝在中原地区连续建都和“一统天下”，被尊为“中央王朝”“中央之国”，进一步奠定了这里政治上的“中国”地位。

在中华民族5000多年文明史上，有3000多年是以河南为国家的政治、经济、文化中心，先后有20多个朝代在此定都；当今中国人口最多的前100个姓氏中，有78个姓氏发源于此；“天下名人，中州过半”，河南也是孕育历史名人最多的省份。以河南为腹地的中原大地如木之根本、水之渊源，在中华民族发展史和中华文明史上具有发端和母体的重要地位，为中华文明起源演进作出了不可磨灭的贡献。

China and East Asia, the Erlitou Culture represents the Bronze Age, when private ownership and classes were in the making, the state was formed, dynasties were founded, and political concepts such as "building the state in the center" were developed. That period marked the emergence of China in the political sense and the beginning of the Chinese civilization.

Later on, different dynasties built their capitals in the Central Plains and ruled the country from there. These "central dynasties" or "central states" further strengthened this region's position as the political center of what we know as China today.

Throughout more than 5,000 years of Chinese history, Henan had served as the political, economic and cultural center for more than 3,000 years as over 20 dynasties chose to build their capitals here. The province is where 78 of the 100 most populous Chinese surnames originated and where the greatest number of historical figures were born. The vast Central Plains with Henan in the center, like the root of a giant tree and the fountainhead of a great river, are the cradle of the Chinese nation and civilization, making indelible contributions to their initiation and evolution.

伏羲

伏羲是中华神话中人类的始祖，华夏民族传说中的三皇五帝之首，华夏文明史纪年符号。伏羲之名最早见于《管子》《荀子》《战国策》等先秦文献。相传其母华胥在雷泽踩了巨大的脚印而有孕，生伏羲于成纪（今甘肃省天水市），定都在陈（今河南省周口市淮阳区）。

相传，伏羲根据天地万物的变化，发明创造了占卜八卦，创造文字，结束了人们“结绳记事”的历史。他又结绳为网，用来捕鸟打猎，教会了人们渔猎的方法，发明了瑟，创作了曲调。伏羲以龙为图腾，将氏族各部落统一起来，进行民族大融合，使龙成为中华民族的图腾和独特精神标识，成为中华文明和中华民族多元一体的象征。伏羲将其统治地域分而治之，而且任命官员进行社会管理，为后代治理社会

Fuxi

In Chinese mythology, Fuxi is the earliest ancestor of humanity and the first of the Three Sovereigns and Five Emperors. He is also a symbol marking the beginning of the Huaxia civilization. The name Fuxi was first seen in the literature of the times before the Qin Dynasty (221-206 BC), such as *Guan Zi* (*The Book of Guan Zi*), *Xun Zi* (*The Book of Xun Zi*) and *Zhan Guo Ce* (*Records on the Warring States*). Legend has it that Fuxi's mother Huaxu conceived him after stepping into a footprint of the God of Thunder and gave birth to him in Chengji (present-day Tianshui, Gansu Province). Fuxi built his capital in Chen (present-day Huaiyang District of Zhoukou, Henan Province).

According to legend, Fuxi created divination and *bagua* (eight trigrams) according to the changes in nature and devised a writing system that ended people's practice of keeping records by tying knots in ropes. He wove nets for catching birds and hunting animals, taught people how to fish and hunt, invented a musical instrument called *se*, and composed tunes for people to play. He united various tribes under the totem of *long* (Chinese dragon), different tribes thus became integrated, and dragon became the symbol of the Chinese nation and civilization. Fuxi divided the territory under his rule and appointed officials to manage them. This provided valuable references for

提供借鉴。伏羲还制定了人类的嫁娶制度，实行男女配偶制，以动物、植物、居所、官职等为姓，防止乱婚和近亲结婚，使中华姓氏自此起源，绵延至今。

河南省至今仍完好保存着的伏羲陵墓——太昊陵，被誉为“天下第一陵”，占地875亩，规模宏大，始建于春秋，历经3000年，祭祀活动绵延不衰。每年的农历二月初二到三月初三，世界各地数百万人前来朝圣，太昊陵庙会成为中国规模最大最古老的民间庙会。

伏羲以其卓著的功绩、肇启文明的伟大贡献，被中华民族推崇为人文始祖、华夏祖先，自古以来就受到历代帝王的尊敬与祭祀，对中华民族的文明进步发挥了重要作用。

later generations in social governance. He also instituted a marriage system, whereby a man would marry a woman as his spouse, and people were surnamed after animals, plants, residences or official titles. This prevented group and consanguineous marriages and started the system of Chinese surnames that has evolved to this day.

The Taihao Mausoleum in Zhoukou, the resting place of Fuxi, is reputed as the "No. 1 tomb in China." First built in the Spring and Autumn Period (770-476 BC), the Mausoleum has survived 3,000 years and still hosts worshipping activities today. Every year, from the second day of the second month to the third day of the third month in the lunar calendar, millions of people from around the world will come here on a pilgrimage, making the Temple Fair of the Taihao Mausoleum the largest and oldest of its kind in China.

Fuxi has been revered by the Chinese nation not only as its own ancestor, but also as the earliest ancestor of humankind for his great contributions to the initiation and development of human society and the Chinese civilization. He was the object of high esteem and devout worship from all Chinese emperors.

炎黄二帝

炎黄二帝是传说中的中国上古帝王炎帝神农氏和黄帝轩辕氏。炎帝是原居姜水流域（今陕西省宝鸡市境内）的部落首领，主要从事农业。黄帝所率领的部落原来过着迁徙无常的游牧生活，后来逐渐在中原地区（今河南省境内）定居下来。在诸多中国史书及神话记载中，华夏文化和中华民族起源于黄河流域的这两个部落，故炎黄二帝被人们称为中华民族的始祖，“炎黄子孙”也就成了中华民族的一个代名词。

炎帝和黄帝对中华民族的生存繁衍和历史人文发展作出了重要贡献。炎帝创造了灿烂的农耕文化，解决了“民以食为天”的大事。农业方面，他驯谷物作为作物品种，发明农具，记录掌握农时，加速原始采集狩猎过渡到种植业；医学方面，他亲尝百草，用草药治病；贸易方面，他促进了原始

Yandi and Huangdi

Yandi (Yan Emperor) and Huangdi (Yellow Emperor) are two legendary rulers in remote antiquity. Yandi, also known as Shennong, was the leader of a tribe farming in the Jiangshui River basin (in present-day Baoji, Shaanxi Province) before migrating to the Central Plains. Huangdi, also known as Xuanyuan, and his tribe first lived a nomadic life, and later they moved to the Central Plains region (present-day Henan Province) and settled there. According to numerous Chinese history books and myths, these two tribes living in the Yellow River basin are the very roots of the Huaxia culture and the Chinese nation, and Yandi and Huangdi are therefore believed to be the earliest ancestors of the Chinese people, who often call themselves "descendants of Yandi and Huangdi," a proud synonym for the entire Chinese nation.

Yandi and Huangdi are said to have made significant contributions to the survival, continuation, and historical and cultural development of the Chinese nation.

Yandi created a brilliant farming culture and thus met the basic need for food of his people. In agriculture, he domesticated wild plants, invented farm tools, recorded the timing for different farming activities, and pushed forward the transition from hunting and gathering to crop planting. In medicine, he tasted all kinds of herbs and used

产品交换的萌芽。黄帝在位期间，治理有方，政治安定，文化制度得到发展。他制定国家的职官制度，创造并实行田亩制，开辟园圃，种植果蔬，种桑养蚕，以蚕丝制衣服；他令仓颉造字，推动文字兴盛。

2007年4月，炎黄二帝巨型塑像在河南省郑州市黄河风景名胜区建成。黄帝故里位于河南省新郑市，是海内外炎黄子孙寻根拜祖的圣地。每年农历三月初三，拜祖大典都会在新郑盛大举办，为传承中华优秀传统文化、增进文化认同、增强民族凝聚力发挥了重要作用。

herbal medicines to treat diseases. In trade, he initiated the primitive form of bartering.

Huangdi achieved political stability and cultural progress during his reign. He instituted the system of officials, invented methods for measuring and distributing the fields to prevent disputes, and led his tribesmen in opening up wasteland to plant vegetables and fruits, grow mulberry and raise silkworms, and use the silk to make clothes. He also asked Cangjie to create a writing system and promoted its use.

In April 2007, huge sculptures of Yandi and Huangdi were erected at the Yellow River Scenic Area in Zhengzhou, capital city of Henan Province. Xinzheng, the birthplace of Huangdi, is a holy place in the hearts of the Chinese people all over the world. The grand ancestor-worshipping ceremony held here on the third day of the third month in the lunar calendar every year plays an irreplaceable role in carrying forward the fine traditional Chinese culture, forging a shared cultural identity, and enhancing national cohesion.

大禹治水

大禹治水是中国古代的神话传说故事。相传，大禹是黄帝的后代。《史记·夏本纪》记载："禹者，黄帝之玄孙而帝颛顼之孙也。"另有史书记载，鲧（禹的父亲）是夏部落首领，大禹也曾被封于"夏地"（今河南禹州市），称为"夏禹国"。

据古籍记载，大约在4000多年前，黄河流域洪水为患，给人民带来了无边的灾难。大禹受命负责治水，他从前人治水实践中汲取经验和教训，把中原大地的山山水水当作一个整体来治理，并发明了疏导治水的新方法。他根据山川地理情况，将中国分为九个州，先治理九州的土地，通过疏通河流、平整土地，使得大片土地变得肥沃；接着治理山路、理通水脉，使田间细水流进大河继而汇入大海。这种变"堵"为"疏"的治理方式体现了古代劳动人民的聪明才智。大禹为了治理洪水，长年在外与各部落人民一起奋战，相传

Da Yu Harnessing the Floods

This is an ancient Chinese myth about Yu, also called Da Yu (Great Yu), who was said to be a descendant of Huangdi. *Shi Ji* (*The Records of the Grand Historian*) records that he was the great-great-grandson of Huangdi and the grandson of Emperor Zhuanxu. Other historical records say that Yu's father Gun was the leader of the Xia tribe and Da Yu was enfeoffed to a place called Xia (present-day Yuzhou, Henan Province), which was known as the State of Xia Yu.

It is recorded in ancient books that more than 4,000 years ago, serious floods in the Yellow River basin inflicted immense disasters upon the local people. Da Yu was entrusted to harness the floods. Drawing lessons from his predecessors, he considered the Central Plains and the numerous mountains and rivers as a whole, and adopted a new dredging approach. Da Yu divided the country into nine parts according to the geographical conditions. He first dredged the rivers and levelled the land to fertilize the soil and then he cut paths through the mountains and cleared the water systems, so the water would flow smoothly into the rivers and then into the sea. This "dredging" rather than "blocking" approach reflected the ingenuity of the ancient people. To harness the floods, Da Yu worked away from home for years in a row alongside the people of different

他曾三过家门而不入。经过13年的奋斗，河水平缓地向东流去，农田变成了粮仓，人民又过上了安居乐业的生活。

大禹治水在中华文明发展史上具有重要意义。大禹作为治理洪水的领导者，躬亲劳苦带领人民栉风沐雨，治水除患，体现了艰苦奋斗、因势利导、科学治水、以人为本的治水理念。治水过程中形成的以公私分明、民族至上、民为根本、科学创新等为内涵的大禹治水精神，成为了中华民族精神的重要象征。

tribes and allegedly passed his home three times without stopping and going in. After 13 years of strenuous efforts, he successfully tamed the floods. The fields became fertile, and the people finally lived in peace.

The story of Da Yu holds a significant position in the history of the Chinese civilization. As the leader of flood control, he worked together with his people braving wind and rain and succeeded by leveraging the local conditions. The spirit formed in this process, which encompasses strict separation between public and private interests, unity among varoius tribes, putting the people first, and rational innovation, has become an essential symbol of the overall spirit of the Chinese nation.

中华姓氏之源

中华姓氏的起源，可以追溯到距今大约5000多年的伏羲时期。姓氏的产生，标志着从群婚制到以血缘关系为基础的婚姻制的转变，成为人类文明进步的一个重要里程碑。

根据中国史籍记载及甲骨文的出现，中国是世界上最早使用姓氏的国家。在《中华姓氏大辞典》中，共列有23813个姓氏，起源于河南省的姓氏共有1834个。按人口数量排在前120位的主要姓氏中，全源于河南省的姓氏有52个，部分源头在河南省的姓氏有45个。无论是李、王、张、刘为代表的“中华四大姓”，还是林、陈、郑、黄为代表的“南方四大姓”，其根源均在河南。

河南省历史悠久，产生的姓氏多。近年来，海外华人华侨持续寻根谒祖，姓氏文化研究方兴未艾。河南省深入考察海外华人姓氏现状及其姓氏宗亲组织，传播了河南省姓氏根亲文化，增强了海外华人“根在中原”的身份认同感。

Origins of Chinese Surnames

Chinese surnames can date back to the time of Fuxi more than 5,000 years ago. The creation of surnames indicated the transition from communal marriage to marriage based on blood relationship, marking a milestone in the evolution of human civilization.

In accordance with Chinese historical records and oracle-bone inscriptions, China is the first country in the world to use surnames. Of the 23,813 surname entries in the *Dictionary of Chinese Surnames*, 1,834 originated in Henan Province. Of the 120 surnames with the most users, 52 originated in Henan fully and 45 partly. The four most populous surnames in China – Li, Wang, Zhang, and Liu – and the four most populous surnames in the southern areas – Lin, Chen, Zheng, and Huang – are all rooted in the province.

The root-seeking efforts of overseas Chinese have revived the studies of the surname culture. Henan's provincial authorities have also conducted in-depth surveys of the current conditions of Chinese surnames and clan organizations overseas. These have preserved Henan's surname culture and enhanced overseas Chinese's identification with their root in the Central Plains.

仰韶文化

仰韶文化是指中国黄河中游地区一种重要的新石器时代彩陶文化，其持续时间大约在公元前5000年至前3000年，分布在整个黄河中游到河南省之间。1921年，因仰韶遗址（今河南省三门峡市境内）发掘而命名的仰韶文化，是中国第一个依靠现代考古学技术、方法和理论而确立的中国史前文化，开启了以科学方法探索和重建中国古史的历程。

仰韶文化是中国分布地域最广、延续长久、内涵丰富的史前文化。彩陶是仰韶文化的重要元素，也是仰韶文化出土器物中最精美的标志。彩陶的大范围传播，被考古学家认为是史前第一次艺术浪潮的代表，其传播至周边多个地区，达到史前艺术的高峰。

仰韶文化遗址不乏特大型中心性聚落，是探索中国早期文明起源的核心地区，是实证中华5000多年文明史的关键区域。距今5300年前后的双槐树遗址（今河南省郑州市境内）作为仰韶文化的核心，是迄今为止在黄河流域仰韶文化

Yangshao Culture

The Yangshao Culture is an important Neolithic painted-pottery culture that existed extensively in the middle reaches of the Yellow River, where Henan Province is located, from 5000 BC to 3000 BC. Named after Yangshao in Sanmenxia, Henan where large cultural deposits were discovered in 1921, it is the first prehistoric culture in China that is confirmed using modern archaeological techniques, methods and theories, marking the beginning of the efforts to explore and rebuild ancient Chinese history with scientific approaches.

The Yangshao Culture features wide distribution, long durance, and significant discoveries. Painted pottery is a crucial element of the culture and the most exquisite representative of the relics of that period. The wide spread of painted pottery to several surrounding regions is considered by archaeologists to be the first artistic surge in prehistoric times.

With several large-scale, concentrated settlements, the Yangshao site is of vital importance for tracing the origin of the Chinese civilization and verifying its 5,000 years of history. The Shuanghuaishu site in Zhengzhou, dating back about 5,300 years, is the center of the Yangshao Culture. Being a city-like central settlement of the highest level among those formed during the middle and late periods of

中晚期即中华文明形成初期发现的规格最高的、具有都邑性质的中心聚落，被誉为“早期中华文明的胚胎”。

仰韶文化的发现，证实了中国存在过较为发达的新石器时代，破除了“中国无石器时代”的谬论，是中国考古史上第一个被正式命名的远古文化体系，对探寻中华文明起源、研究中华民族多元一体演进格局具有重要意义。

the Yangshao Culture, or the initial period of the Chinese civilization, the site is reputed as the embryo of the Chinese civilization.

The discovery of the Yangshao Culture proves the existence of a highly developed Neolithic Age in China and disproves the fallacy that "there was no Stone Age in China." The Yangshao Culture, as the first ancient cultural system to have an official name in China's archaeological history, is significant for tracing the origin of the Chinese civilization and studying the integrated evolution of the Chinese nation in diversity.

河洛文化

河洛地区是黄河与洛水相交汇的广大区域。河洛文化即以河洛地区为中心、从上古时期至北宋时期的传统文化。

在河洛大地上，从新石器时代早期的裴李岗文化（距今约8000年）开始，到仰韶文化、河南龙山文化，再到夏文化，连绵不绝，一脉相承。其国都文化连绵不断，中国古代的许多重要都城均在河洛文化圈内。河洛文化博大精深，内涵丰富，以“河图洛书”为标志，以夏商周文化为主干，以汉魏唐宋为内容，以古都洛阳所凝聚的文化精华为核心，以“河洛郎”为特征，文化传承范围广泛，文化内涵不断丰富延伸。

河洛文化是中华文明的摇篮文化，是数千年来中国传统文化的主体，因而在中国古代文化史上举足轻重。河洛文化强化了世界华夏儿女对中华传统文化的认同感，是海内外华人的民族血脉和精神纽带，具有显著的源头性、根脉性。2020年，中国设立了“河洛文化生态保护实验区”，以保护非物质文化遗产为核心加强河洛文化生态保护。

Heluo Culture

The Heluo region is the area where the Yellow River meets the Luoshui River, and the Heluo culture refers to the mainstream culture prevailing at this confluence that spanned a long period from time immemorial to the Northern Song Dynasty (960-1126).

The Heluo region is the cradle of a continuous stream of ancient cultures, from the Peiligang Culture in the early Neolithic Age (about 8,000 years ago) to the Yangshao Culture, the Longshan Culture, and the Xia Culture, with many capital cities built here. The rich and profound Heluo culture has a wealth of highlights, such as *Hetu* and *Luoshu*, the cultures of the Xia, the Shang, and the Zhou dynasties all the way to the Han, the Wei, the Tang, and the Song dynasties, the amazing city of Luoyang that served as the capital of multiple dynasties, and the Heluo migrants to Fujian Province and other places in southern China. They have enriched the Heluo culture in breadth and depth.

As the cradle of the Chinese civilization and the backbone of the traditional Chinese culture, the Heluo culture occupies a pivotal position in China's cultural history. It helps enhance the Chinese people's identification with their traditional culture and holds them together with a shared cultural root. In 2020, an experimental zone was set up for ecological protection of the Heluo culture as an intangible cultural heritage.

木兰文化

花木兰是中国古代传说的四大巾帼英雄之一，最早出现于南北朝的叙事诗《木兰辞》中，后在民间广为流传。北魏太武年间（公元424年至452年），中国北方游牧民族不断南下侵扰，北魏政权规定每家派出一名男子上前线。但木兰父亲年迈、体弱多病，弟弟幼小无法参军，于是木兰替父从军，驻守边关，既要英勇作战，又要隐瞒性别，克服了难以想象的艰难。十多年后，木兰凯旋，皇帝欲加官进爵，木兰却毅然拒绝，返乡孝敬父母，后被唐朝皇帝追封为“孝烈将军”。

现河南省虞城县存有始建于唐朝的木兰祠。祠中设木兰像，并存有元朝《孝烈将军祠像辨正记》碑和清朝《孝烈将军辨误正名记》碑两块祠碑。2007年，中国民间文艺家协

Hua Mulan

Hua Mulan is one of the most known heroines in Chinese folklore. Her name first appeared in a narrative poem, *Mu Lan Ci* (*The Ballad of Mulan*), of the Northern and Southern Dynasties (420-589) and became a household name later. It was said that during the reign of Emperor Taiwu of the Northern Wei Dynasty in the fifth century, the northern nomadic groups constantly invaded southward, and the Northern Wei emperor demanded that each household send a male to fight on the frontline. Having a sick old father and a little brother too young to go, Hua Mulan joined the army in her father's place. She battled gallantly on the frontier while trying her best to hide her female identity. A dozen years later, she came back in triumph. She declined the emperor's offer of promotion and returned home to fulfill her filial duty to her parents.

Hua Mulan was posthumously honored as General of Filial Piety and Military Prowess in the Tang Dynasty (618-907), and a temple was built to commemorate her. Still standing in Yucheng County of Henan Province today, the temple houses a statue of the heroine and two steles, one established in the Yuan Dynasty (1279-1368) and the other in the Qing Dynasty (1644-1911), that record her origin, hometown, time, and military exploits. In 2007, the China Folk Literature and Art Association officially confirmed

会正式命名虞城县为“中国木兰之乡”。2008年，《木兰传说》入选国家级非物质文化遗产名录。

千百年来，花木兰已经成为中华女性杰出代表和民族精神的化身，其所代表的以家国情怀为核心的忠孝节义、勇武仁爱的精神，激励着一代代中华儿女。木兰文化涉及伦理、民俗、宗教、文学、艺术等多方面内容，具有珍贵的历史研究价值。描写和讴歌木兰动人事迹的诗歌、游记、散文等作品广为流传，曾上演过木兰戏的剧种包括京剧、豫剧、越剧、昆曲、秦腔、黄梅戏等20多种。木兰故事在日本、韩国、朝鲜早有流传，并且以多种艺术形式传播到欧美国家。《木兰辞》英译本最早见于1880年由伦敦特鲁伯纳公司和上海别发印书局同时出版的《翰林文稿：中国人智慧生活文录》一书。美国迪士尼电影公司分别于1998年和2004年推出两部《花木兰》动画片，并于2020年推出真人版3D电影《花木兰》。木兰文化的海外传播，融入了世界各国人民对其精神内涵的理解，促进了中外文化交流。

Yucheng County as the hometown of Hua Mulan. In 2008, the legend of Hua Mulan was included in the national list of intangible cultural heritage.

Through the ages, Hua Mulan has been a representative of outstanding Chinese women and the incarnation of the Chinse ethos. Her loyalty, filial piety, bravery, and courage, all growing out of a deep love for the family and the country, have inspired generations of Chinese. The culture related to Hua Mulan is a valuable asset for historical studies as it involves ethics, folklore, religion, literature, and art. Literary works including poems, travel notes, and prose in honor of the ancient heroine are widely circulated, and her stories have been staged in more than 20 Chinese opera genres, such as Peking, Henan, Yueju, Kunqu, Qinqiang and Huangmei operas.

The stories of Hua Mulan have long spread to Japan and the Korean Peninsular and been taken to Europe and America in a number of art forms. The earliest English translation of *The Ballad of Mulan* appeared in a book titled *Hanlin Papers or Essays on the Intellectual Life of the Chinese* published by Trubner & Co. of London and Kelly & Walsh of Shanghai in 1880. In 1998 and 2004, the Walt Disney Company produced two animated movies *Mulan* about the heroine, followed by a live-action 3D movie of the same title in 2020. The overseas circulation of the stories of Hua Mulan has taken in the foreign audience's understanding of her spirit and promoted cultural exchanges between China and the rest of the world.

愚公移山

愚公移山是中国家喻户晓的寓言故事。战国时期思想家、哲学家列子以流传在太行、王屋山区（今河南济源）的民间故事为原型，创作了《愚公移山》，收录在《列子 · 汤问》中。

相传北山山下住着一位名叫愚公的老人。他的家门南面有两座大山挡住出路，一座叫太行山，一座叫王屋山。愚公下决心要挖走这两座大山，率领儿子们凿石挖土。有位名叫智叟的老人讥笑愚公一家的行为太愚蠢了，认为仅凭愚公父子几人要挖掉两座大山是完全不可能的。愚公回答说："我虽然老了，但我死后有我的儿子，还有孙子，子子孙孙是没有穷尽的。这两座高山却不会再增高了，挖一点就会少一点，怎么会挖不平呢？"春去秋来，愚公移山的意志不变，日夜搬山不止。愚公的坚持感动了天帝，他派两个神仙下凡，背走了那两座山，帮助愚公实现了移山通路的理想。

The Old Man Yu Gong Moving the Mountains

This is a household fable in China. Lie Zi, a thinker and philosopher of the Warring States Period (475-221 BC), created this story based on folk tales popular in the areas near the Taihang and the Wangwu mountains in present-day Jiyuan, Henan Province, which was included in *Lie Zi* (*The Book of Lie Zi*).

Legend has it that once upon a time, there lived an old man, called Yu Gong ("foolish old man"), near the two great mountains – Taihang and Wangwu. As these two mountains blocked the way of his family to the south, Yu Gong decided to have them removed with the support of his sons. Their effort, however, was ridiculed by another old man, Zhi Sou ("wise old man"), who called the family "foolish" and their mission "impossible." Yu Gong replied, "I may be old, but after I die, my sons and grandsons will carry on, followed by their sons and grandsons, and so on to infinity. These two mountains, however, will not grow any taller. As long as we keep digging the earth and rocks away bit by bit, the day will eventually come when they are completely removed." Time flew, and Yu Gong kept on working day and night as determined as ever. His persistence moved the Heavenly Emperor, who dispatched two immortals to carry the two mountains away and thus helped Yu Gong realize his dream of having an unblocked way leading to the outside world.

千百年来，愚公移山的故事为人们代代传颂、反复解读，成为中华文化史上独具特色的智慧故事。愚公移山精神作为中华优秀传统文化的重要标识，蕴含深刻内涵：其一，志存高远，改造世界，实现大道之行，天下为公；其二，务实重干，勇毅前行，做到大道至简，实干为要；其三，万众一心，团结互助，实现大道不孤，天下一家。这一精神激励着当代中国人团结奋进，为实现中华民族伟大复兴的中国梦而努力奋斗。

For centuries, the story of Yu Gong has been passed down from generation to generation. His spirit, as an important symbol of the fine traditional Chinese culture, lends some deep insights. First, one needs to aim high to transform the world so that it will benefit all. Second, one needs to press ahead with fortitude in the belief that great visions, simple though, can come true through solid actions. Third, people need to support each other and build the world into one big family. The perseverance of Yu Gong is still inspiring contemporary Chinese to realize the Chinese Dream of national rejuvenation through hard work together.

二十四节气

二十四节气是中国历法中表示自然节律变化的特定节令。中国古人将一岁分为四时，即春、夏、秋、冬各3个月，每月2个节气，一年共有24个节气：立春、雨水、惊蛰、春分、清明、谷雨、立夏、小满、芒种、夏至、小暑、大暑、立秋、处暑、白露、秋分、寒露、霜降、立冬、小雪、大雪、冬至、小寒、大寒，每个节气均有其独特的含义。

二十四节气形成于中国黄河流域，自西周开始，至今已沿用2000多年。河南省登封市观星台是二十四节气产生的最直接文物史证，现存有700年历史的“量天尺”，用来测量正午日影，可定节气和一年时长。观星台由元朝著名天文

The Twenty-Four Solar Terms

The 24 solar terms are the 24 days in the Chinese calendar that indicate the seasonal division points and movement of the natural cycle. The ancient Chinese divided a year into four seasons – spring, summer, autumn, and winter, each lasting three months and each month having two solar terms, which make up 24 terms for the whole year. The 24 solar terms are: Beginning of Spring, Rain Water, Awakening of Insects, Spring Equinox, Pure Brightness, Grain Rain, Beginning of Summer, Grain Budding, Grain in Ear, Summer Solstice, Slight Heat, Great Heat, Beginning of Autumn, End of Heat, White Dew, Autumn Equinox, Cold Dew, Frost's Descent, Beginning of Winter, Light Snow, Heavy Snow, Winter Solstice, Slight Cold, and Great Cold. Each term denotes a natural phenomenon with phenological meanings.

The 24 solar terms were created in the Yellow River basin and have been in use for more than 2,000 years since the Western Zhou Dynasty (1046-771 BC). The Astronomical Observatory in Dengfeng, Henan Province is a direct proof of China's invention of the 24 solar terms, as its Sky Measuring Scale, which has a history of 700 years, is a device used to measure the shadow cast by the sun at noon and consequently determine when a solar term falls and how many days a year has. The observatory was

学家郭守敬主持建造，他在此准确地测定出一年中有二十四个节气，用以指导生产生活。

二十四节气不仅是指导农耕生产的时节体系，更是包含丰富民俗事象的文化系统。作为中华优秀传统文化的重要组成部分，二十四节气曾传播到朝鲜、日本、越南等国家，对当地农耕生产和社会文化发展产生了积极影响。2016年11月，二十四节气被列入联合国教科文组织“人类非物质文化遗产代表作名录”。

built under the direction of Guo Shoujing, a renowned astronomer in the Yuan Dynasty. Guo used it to accurately identify the 24 solar terms and direct the farming and daily routines.

The 24 solar terms constitute not only a system of seasonal changes that guides farming, but also a cultural system involving a diversity of folklore and customs. As a major part of the fine traditional Chinese culture, they have been introduced to the Korean Peninsular, Japan, Vietnam, and other places and exerted positive effects on their agrarian production and social and cultural development. In November 2016, the 24 solar terms were inscribed on the UNESCO's Representative List of the Intangible Cultural Heritage of Humanity.

河图洛书

河图洛书是中国古代流传下来的两幅神秘图案，是中华文化、阴阳五行术数之源。传说伏羲时期，有龙马从黄河出现，背负“河图”；有神龟从洛水出现，背负“洛书”。伏羲根据该“图”“书”画成八卦，就是后来《周易》的来源。但现代科学一般认为它们是远古时代人民按照星象排布出时间、方向和季节的辨别系统，蕴含了深奥的宇宙星象之理，因而将它们誉为“宇宙魔方”。

河图和洛书分别是中国古代的天文与地理方位图，被广泛应用于中国古代科技。这两幅图包含着基本的自然数之间的算数逻辑关系，两者之间有着必然内在联系。河图的“河”指的是银河。河图最初的原型是一条白色旋转的龙，将银河画成白龙，围绕着中点运转，而这个中点是北极星。这幅图在后来演变成了一黑一白两条龙，逐渐成为

Hetu and *Luoshu*

Hetu (Yellow River Chart) and *Luoshu* (Luoshui River Script) are two mysterious diagrams passed down from the ancient times as the origin of the Chinese culture and the theories of *yin-yang* and five elements. Legend has it that in the period of Fuxi, a dragon horse surfaced in the Yellow River carrying on its back a mysterious diagram, known as *Hetu*, while a turtle surfaced in the Luoshui River carrying the other, *Luoshu*. Fuxi drew up *bagua*, or the eight trigrams, based on the two diagrams, which became the basis of *Zhou Yi* (*Changes of Zhou*) written later. In modern times, *Hetu* and *Luoshu* are generally believed to be the astronomical systems invented by the ancient Chinese to identify time, directions, and seasons. They are called the "magic cube of the universe" for the patterns of the universe and the stars and the profound principles contained therein.

Hetu and *Luoshu*, one being an astronomical diagram and the other a geographical one, were widely used in ancient Chinese science and technology. Both containing basic arithmetical logic, they are inherently linked. The *He* in *Hetu* actually refers to the galaxy, which was originally designed like a white dragon revolving around a central point – the North Star. Later this diagram evolved into two dragons, one black and the other white, and gradually became the Taiji Diagram familiar to the people of today.

了今人熟悉的太极阴阳图。洛书是脉络图，是表述天地空间变化脉络的图案，包括水平空间、二维空间，以及东西南北四个方向。

河图洛书的影响体现在中国传统文化的各个领域，汉语中的“图书”“图书馆”等词汇就源于此。2014年11月，河图洛书传说被列入中国国家级非物质文化遗产。

Luoshu outlines the changes of heaven and earth and everything in between, including the horizontal space, the two-dimensional space, and the four directions.

Hetu and *Luoshu* have exerted great influence on the traditional Chinese culture. For instance, the Chinese words like *tushu* (book) and *tushuguan* (library) have stemmed from them. In November 2014, the legend of *Hetu* and *Luoshu* became a national intangible cultural heritage of China.

《说文解字》

《说文解字》是一部语文工具书。其作者许慎是汝南召陵（今河南省漯河市）人，东汉著名经学家、文字学家、语言学家，中国文字学的开拓者，后人尊称其为“字圣”。

《说文解字》是中国最早系统分析汉字字形和考究字源的语文辞书。这本书从上万个汉字中，把它们的偏旁和部首区别出来，归纳为540个部首，开创了按部首编排汉字的方法。直至今日，中国人使用的汉语字典、词典仍然使用部首检字法编排。

《说文解字》共15卷，其中前14卷为文字解说，对造字法做出了具体说明，并解释字形与字义或字音之间的关系。第15卷为叙目，记录汉字的产生、发展、功用、结构等，以及作者创作的目的。全书共收录汉字9353个，另有“重文”（即异体字）1163个，共10516字。

Shuo Wen Jie Zi

Shuo Wen Jie Zi (*An Analytical Dictionary of Chinese Characters*), is a reference book for the study of Chinese characters. It was compiled by Xu Shen (58-147), an established scholar and linguist of the Eastern Han Dynasty (25-220). Born in Zhaoling, Runan (present-day Luohe, Henan Province), Xu is a trailblazer of Chinese characters, who has been esteemed as the "Sage of Characters" by later generations.

Shuo Wen Jie Zi is the first dictionary that systematically analyzes the structure and etymology of Chinese characters. It categorizes over 10,000 characters into 540 sections under different radicals, according to which the characters are arranged and sequenced. This method is still used in Chinese dictionaries today.

The book consists of 15 chapters. The first 14 chapters are character entries that explain in detail why and how the characters are so formed and how the form is related to the meaning or pronunciation. The 15th chapter is a postface that records the emergence, development, usage, and structure of characters, as well as the purpose of the author in compiling the book. There are altogether 9,353 character entries, plus 1,163 graphic variants, totaling 10,516 characters.

《说文解字》是中国语言学史上第一部分析字形、说解字义、辨识声读的字典，被誉为“科学文字学和文献语言学的奠基之作”。《说文解字》还是记录自然和历史文化的百科全书，其中保留的大量古代历史、文化方面的材料，有助于世人了解中国古代历史和语言文化发展。

Shuo Wen Jie Zi is the first dictionary in the Chinese history of linguistics that analyzes the structure of characters, explains their meanings, and identifies their sounds, being reputed as the "cornerstone treatise on characters and philology." It is also an encyclopedia that helps people understand China's ancient history and linguistic and cultural evolution.

《易经》

《易经》是阐述天地世间万象变化的古老经典，也是博大精深的辩证法哲学书。《易经》包括《连山》《归藏》《周易》三部经书，其中《连山》《归藏》已经失传，现存于世的只有《周易》。相传伏羲根据河图洛书画成八卦，即为《周易》之来源。

《易经》记录了中国古人探索宇宙奥秘，并由此演绎出的一套完整深奥的星象推理文化，内容涉及哲学、政治、生活、文学、艺术、科学等诸多领域。上古时期，中国古人观察天象，确定天干地支、阴阳五行、八卦原理，结合时空、阴阳观念，发展成为一个系统的世界观，用阴阳、乾坤、刚柔的对立统一来解释宇宙万物和人类社会的一切变化。《易经》反映了中国古人对宇宙万物时刻变化的认识，揭示了宇宙的特性，囊括了天地间万物的发展属性。

在中国历史上，《易经》被誉为诸经之首，是中国传

Yi Jing

Yi Jing (*The Book of Changes*) is an ancient classic expounding the changes of the universe and everything in it. It is also an enigmatic philosophical treatise on dialectics. The original *Yi Jing* consists of three volumes, but only one of them – *Zhou Yi* – is extant today, which, as legend has it, stems from the eight trigrams drawn by Fuxi based on *Hetu* and *Luoshu*.

Yi Jing records a complete set of profound astrological reasoning developed by the ancient Chinese through the observation of the universe and covers a wide range of subjects including philosophy, politics, life, literature, arts, and science. In remote ancient times, the Chinese people formulated such concepts as *tiangan* (Heavenly Stems) and *dizhi* (Earthly Branches), *yin* and *yang*, five elements, and *bagua* by observing the movement of celestial bodies. Based on that, they developed a systematic worldview that explained all beings in the universe and all changes in human society according to the principle of unity of the opposites, such as *yin* and *yang*, *qian* (heaven) and *kun* (earth), and hardness and softness. The book reflects how the ancient Chinese understood the perpetual changes of the universe, reveals its features and traits, and depicts how everything between heaven and earth evolves.

Regarded as the first of all classics in Chinese history,

统思想文化中自然哲学与人文实践的理论根源，为古代政治家、军事家、学者、商业家所推崇。经过不断演绎，《易经》已成为一门哲学，描述了中国人遵循的一种“天人合一”自然生存法则，并孕育了中华民族自强不息、厚德载物的民族精神。

Yi Jing is held in high esteem by the ancient statesmen, military strategists, scholars, and businessmen alike as the theoretical root for the natural philosophy and cultural practices contained in traditional Chinese thinking. Through constant evolution and improvement, the ideas expressed in the book have become a philosophy. It explains the rule of living followed by the Chinese known as "man is an integral part of nature" and gives birth to the spirit of the Chinese nation – striving continuously for self-improvement and caring for all things with ample virtue.

儒释道

儒、释、道是中国传统文化的主要思想来源和精髓。

儒文化与起源于河南省商丘市，兴盛于河南省安阳市的殷商文化一脉相承。周初时期，那些自觉保留了殷商文明的前朝遗民开始被称为“儒”。殷商末期的箕子撰写的《洪范》是中国古代政治哲学的重要奠基著作，其中的五行学说、天人感应学说、王道学说可称为儒学的先驱；春秋时期鲁国孔子借鉴丰富的上古文化资源，创建了以“道德仁义”为宗旨、以“礼乐正名”为特色的儒家思想体系。

“释”是古印度（今尼泊尔境内）释迦牟尼创立的佛教，故又称释教，为世界三大宗教之一，主张众生平等和因果报应。自汉朝传入中国后，佛教同中国传统文化相融合。始建

Confucianism, Buddhism, and Daoism

Confucianism, Buddhism, and Daoism represent the main philosophical sources and essence of the traditional Chinese culture.

Confucianism, or "*rujia*" in Chinese, came down in one continuous line with the Shang culture that originated in Shangqiu and bloomed in Anyang, both in Henan. In the early period of the Western Zhou Dynasty, the adherents of the preceding Shang Dynasty who consciously retained the Shang culture were called *ru*. Ji Zi, a man of the late Shang Dynasty, authored a masterpiece of political philosophy, *Hong Fan* (*The Grand Rules*). The theories of the five elements, of nature and man responding to each other, and of the Kingly Way (benevolent governance), which he elaborated on in the book, could be considered the precursors of Confucianism, or the school of the *ru*. In the Spring and Autumn Period, Confucius (551-479 BC), a thinker and educator from the State of Lu, drew on the rich ancient culture and established Confucianism that valued virtue, benevolence, justice, and a rigorous system of norms centering on rituals and music.

Buddhism, created by Sakyamuni of a kingdom in ancient India (in present-day Nepal), is one of the three main religions in the world. It advocates equality of all and karma. Buddhism spread to China in the Han Dynasty

于东汉永平十一年（公元68年）的洛阳白马寺是佛教传入中国后兴建的第一座官办寺院，也因此被认为是中国佛教的发源地，有中国佛教的“祖庭”和“释源”之称。

“道”是以黄老学派“清静无为”思想为基础形成的哲学思想体系，起源于战国时期。汉武帝后，黄老学说走向民间，与方仙道合流，由张道陵创立了五斗米道，奉老子为教祖并尊称其为“太上老君”。位于河南省洛阳市栾川县的老君山，距今已有两千多年人文历史，是道教中历史最长的山脉。春秋时期，被公认为道教始祖的老子李耳到此归隐修炼，使之成为“道源”（道教起源地）和“祖庭”（祖师之庭）。

秦汉以后，中国传统文化的主流基本是儒释道三家。元末明初，儒释道三家进一步融合发展，形成“三教合一”。其中儒家修身“治世”，作为一种治理国家的意识形态曾长期作为中国官方意识形态，确立了中国传统社会的礼仪规范

(206 BC-AD 220) and blended with the traditional Chinese culture. The Baima Temple in Luoyang built in 68 was the first government-funded Buddhist temple in the country, and therefore it is regarded as the ancestral chamber and place of origin of Chinese Buddhism.

Daoism is a philosophical system originating in the Warring States Period. It is based on the principles established by the philosophical school of Huangdi and Lao Zi (dates unknown), such as seeking peace of mind and non-action. After Emperor Wu's reign (141-87 BC) in the Han Dynasty, Huang-Lao teachings caught on among the common people and blended with folk beliefs and immortal alchemy. Later, Zhang Daoling (34-156) created the Wudoumi sect of Daoism, which worshipped Lao Zi as their religious ancestor and honored him as the supreme deity. The Laojun Mountain in Henan's Luanchuan County has more than 2,000 years of history associated with Daoism. It is considered the cradle and ancestral place of Daoism because Lao Zi, who was generally believed to be the founder of Daoism, had lived here in seclusion for self-cultivation.

Confucianism, Buddhism, and Daoism had represented the mainstream traditional Chinese culture ever since the Han Dynasty, and they further integrated in the late Yuan and early Ming (1368-1644) dynasties.

Confucianism, which encourages self-cultivation and contribution to good governance, for a long time was upheld as China's official philosophy in state governance,

与典章制度，其影响波及朝鲜半岛、日本、中亚、东南亚地区；道家养性“治身”，强调“道法自然”，认为人应该顺应自然规律，追求内心的平静和自由；佛家修心“治心”，主张通过内心的修行和觉悟来消除痛苦和不满。三家既相互竞争，又彼此吸收融合，共同构成了中国传统社会的处世和哲学基础。

with rituals and rules established in ancient Chinese society. It has also exerted great influences on the Korean Peninsula, Japan, Central Asia, and Southeast Asia. Daoism advocates nourishing one's nature and emphasizes that *dao*, or the Way, follows nature, meaning letting things take their natural course. It holds that people should follow the natural laws and pursue inner quietude and freedom. Buddhism, on the other hand, urges people to relieve themselves of misery and discontent by cultivating the heart and attaining enlightenment. The three schools of thoughts competed and assimilated with each other at the same time, jointly constituting the philosophy of life in traditional Chinese society.

老子

老子，姓李名耳，相传为春秋时期陈国（今河南省周口市鹿邑县）人，著名思想家与哲学家，道家学派创始人和主要代表，被尊为“道祖”，入选“世界百位历史名人”。

老子建立了以“道”为中心的学说，认为“道”是天地万物的根源，“德”是事物自身的本性，“道”为体、“德”为用。老子思想的核心是朴素辩证法，认为世界上的任何事物都是相比较而存在的，相互对立的两个方面实际上是相互包含、相互渗透的，即“你中有我，我中有你”，并非一成不变。他在政治上主张小国寡民、无为而治，在修身方面讲求虚心实腹、不与人争的修持。

老子所著的《道德经》，以哲学意义之“道德”为纲宗，论述修身、治国、用兵、养生之道，文意深奥，内涵广博，

Lao Zi

Lao Zi, whose real name is Li Er, is a renowned Chinese thinker and philosopher. Allegedly born in the State of Chen (present-day Luyi County of Zhoukou, Henan Province) in the Spring and Autumn Period, he is the founder and chief representative of Daoism and is revered as the Daoist progenitor. He is included in *The 100: A Ranking of the Most Influential Persons in History*.

Lao Zi created theories centered on *dao* (the Way). He believed that *dao* is the origin of all things in the universe while *de* (virtue) is their inherent nature, the former being the essence and the latter being the manifestation. The core of Lao Zi's theories is naive dialectics. He held that everything in the world exists by comparison and two opposing aspects are actually interconnected and permeate each other through constant changes. Politically, Lao Zi advocated small states with small populations and governance through non-action; and personally, he advocated controlling one's desires, remaining indifferent to worldly gain, and not contending with others.

Dao De Jing (*Classic of the Way and Virtue*), authored by Lao Zi, is centered on *dao* and *de* in their philosophical sense. It is a wide-ranging, recondite monograph on the principles of self-cultivation, state governance, deployment of troops, and physical fitness, exerting profound influences

对中国传统哲学、科学、政治、宗教等领域产生了深刻影响，还被译为几十种文字在世界范围内传播，成为全人类的宝贵精神财富。

老子的“道法自然”“无为而无不为”“上善若水”“以百姓心为心”等学说，深刻影响着中国人的哲学观念和思维方式。河南省周口市鹿邑县设有纪念老子的太清宫和传承与弘扬老子学说的“老子学院”，被称为“中国老子文化之乡”。

on China's traditional philosophy, science, politics, and religions. It has been translated into dozens of languages and circulated all over the world as a valuable cultural asset of humanity.

Many of Lao Zi's ideas, such as "letting things take their natural course," "action through non-action," "great virtue is like water," and "doing what the people wish," have immensely influenced Chinese people's philosophical concepts and way of thinking. A Taiqing Palace (Palace of Heaven) in memorial of Lao Zi and a Lao Zi Institute advocating his theories are built in Luyi County, the hometown of Daoist culture.

庄子

庄子（约公元前369年—约公元前286年），姓庄名周，出生于战国时期宋国蒙邑（今河南省商丘市），著名思想家、哲学家和文学家，是继老子之后道家学派的主要代表人物，与老子并称“老庄”。

“道”是庄子思想的核心。庄子继承和发展了老子的“道法自然”学说。庄子的“道”是天道，是效法自然的“道”。他主张顺从“天道”，而摒弃“人为”，把“道”和人紧密结合，使“道”成为人生所要达到的最高境界。庄子思想蕴含着朴素辩证法以及相对论认知，其自然原则是和相对主义联系在一起的。他认为，事物总是相对而又相生的，也就是说任何事物都具有既互相对立，又互相依赖的正反两个方面，事物的变化总是向其对立的方面转化。

庄子著说十余万字，大多都是寓言，收录于《庄子》中。《庄子》一书想象奇幻，构思巧妙，用寓言故事表达哲学主张，把微妙难言的哲理写得引人入胜，乃先秦诸子文章的典范之作，对中国哲学思想和文学艺术发展产生深远影响。

Zhuang Zi

Zhuang Zi (369-286 BC), whose real name is Zhuang Zhou, is a renowned thinker, philosopher, and litterateur. Born in Mengyi (present-day Shangqiu, Henan Province) in the Warring States Period, he is a chief representative of Daoism after Lao Zi, and the two of them are often collectively referred to as "Lao-Zhuang."

The core of Zhuang Zi's thinking is *dao*. He further developed Lao Zi's idea that *dao* follows nature and advocated that people should follow *dao* of nature and heaven, minimize human interference, and strive to attain *dao* as the ultimate realm of personal achievement. Zhuang Zi's ideas contain naive dialectics and the theory of relativity. He believed that things are always conflicting and mutually promoting, that everything contains two opposing yet interdependent aspects, and that things always evolve toward their opposites.

Zhuang Zi's writings, immense in quantity and mostly fables and allegories, are collected in an eponymous treatise. *Zhuang Zi* is a well-conceived, widely imaginative illustration of subtle and abstract philosophical assertions written in an apprehensible and engrossing way. A paradigm of articles by pre-Qin thinkers and philosophers, the book has left far-reaching influences on the development of Chinese philosophy, literature, and art.

张仲景

张仲景（约公元150～154年—约公元215～219年），名机，字仲景，东汉末年南阳郡（今河南省南阳市）人，著名医学家，被后人尊称为“医圣”。

东汉时期，南阳地区接连发生瘟疫，许多人因此丧生，其中尤以死于伤寒病的人最多。张仲景内心十分悲愤，便痛下决心，潜心研究伤寒病的诊治。经过数十年含辛茹苦的努力，张仲景终于写成《伤寒杂病论》，论述了分析病情、认识证候及临床治疗的“辨证施治”原则。这一原则不仅为诊疗一切外感热病提出了纲领性的法则，同时也给中医临床各科找出了诊疗规律，成为指导后世医家临床实践的基本原则。

《伤寒杂病论》集秦汉以来医药理论之大成，并广泛应用于医疗实践，是中国医学史上影响深远的中医学典籍之一，也是中国第一部临床治疗学方面的巨著，成为后学者研习中医必备的经典著作。

Zhang Zhongjing

Zhang Zhongjing (c. 150-c. 219), also named Zhang Ji, is a preeminent Chinese doctor from Nanyang (present-day Nanyang, Henan Province) of the late Eastern Han Dynasty. He is revered as the "Sage of Chinese Medicine" by later generations.

In Zhang Zhongjing's time, constant plagues in Nanyang cost many lives, most of whom died from typhoid fever. Grieved by the people's misery, Zhang made up his mind to delve into the diagnosis and treatment of the disease. After decades of hard work, he completed *Shang Han Za Bing Lun* (*Treatise on Cold Pathogenic and Miscellaneous Diseases*), a comprehensive treatise on traditional Chinese medicine (TCM) that established the principle of applying clinical treatment based on accurate identification of symptoms and careful analysis of the disease. This became the guideline for diagnosing and treating all fever-related diseases, benefiting TCM practitioners of later ages..

Shang Han Za Bing Lun is a masterpiece encompassing the medical and pharmacological theories of the Qin and the Han dynasties, which have been widely used in medical practices. It is a TCM classic of far-reaching influences, China's first monograph on clinical treatment, and a go-to reference for TCM learners.

张仲景的医学理论对中国古代医学的发展和百姓健康作出了巨大贡献，并对现代医学研究作出重大贡献，深刻影响朝鲜、越南、印度尼西亚、新加坡、蒙古国等国的医学发展。后人研究张仲景的医理，敬仰其医术和医德，在河南省南阳市为其修建了“医圣祠”。

Zhang Zhongjing's medical theories made great contributions to the medical development and people's health in ancient China as well as to modern medical research. They have also exerted immense influences on the medical development of the Korean Peninsular, Vietnam, Indonesia, Singapore, and Mongolia. A Temple of the Medical Sage is built in Nanyang in honor of Zhang for his medical expertise and professional ethics.

玄奘

玄奘（公元602年—公元664年），姓陈名祎，唐朝高僧，河南洛州（今河南省洛阳市）人，中国汉传佛教四大佛经翻译家之一，中国汉传佛教唯识宗创始人。

玄奘从小学习各种佛法，因为感到各师所说不一，各种经典也不尽相同，于是决定西行求法，以解迷惑。公元629年，玄奘从长安出发，历经千难万险，后入天竺，诚心求学问贤，于公元645年携佛经佛像等抵达故土。公元648年，大慈恩寺落成，玄奘被任命为该寺的首任住持。在此后的十几年时间里，玄奘专心致志地翻译那些他从天竺带回的佛经。直至去世前，玄奘和他的弟子们一共翻译佛经75部1335卷，计1300万言。其所译经籍对丰富中国宗教文化作出了巨大贡献，并为古印度佛教保存了珍贵的典籍。此

Xuanzang

Xuanzang (602-664), whose name is Chen Yi, is an eminent monk from Luozhou (present-day Luoyang, Henan Province) of the Tang Dynasty. He is one of the four great translators of Buddhist scriptures into Chinese language, and he founded the Weishi sect of Chinese Buddhism.

Xuanzang learned Buddhist scriptures at an early age. Bewildered by the discrepancies in different versions of scripture texts, he decided to travel to India in search of authentic Buddhist sutras. He set out from Chang'an, the capital city, in 629 and, after enduring tremendous difficulties and hardships, arrived in Tianzhu (present-day India) to study from Buddhist sages. In 645, Xuanzang came back to China with a large number of Buddhist scriptures and statues.

In 648, he was appointed the first abbot of the newly built Daci'en Temple (Temple of Mercy and Kindness), where he spent more than 10 years translating the scriptures he brought back. Before he passed away, Xuanzang and his disciples had translated 75 scriptures running to 1,335 rolls, totalling 13 million words, not only preserving precious classics for ancient Indian Buddhism, but also greatly enriching the religious culture in China.

Xuanzang recorded his experiences in the Western Regions and India in a travelogue titled *Da Tang Xi Yu*

外，玄奘还将其在西域和印度的亲历见闻撰写成《大唐西域记》，为研究中国西北地区及印度、尼泊尔、中亚等地民间传说、文学与文化提供了重要材料。以玄奘西行为蓝本创作的著名古典小说《西游记》，被列为中国古代四大名著之一。

Ji (*Great Tang Records on the Western Regions*), which provides important references for the study of the folklore, literature, and culture in northwest China, India, Nepal, and Central Asia. The famous novel *Xi You Ji* (*Journey to the West*), authored by Wu Cheng'en (c. 1500-c. 1582), is based on Xuanzang's personal experiences and regarded as one of the four great classic novels of Chinese literature.

杜甫

杜甫（公元712年—公元770年），字子美，河南巩县（今河南省巩义市）人，唐朝伟大的现实主义诗人，被称为“诗圣”，其诗被称为“诗史”，共有约1500首诗歌被保留下来。

杜甫生活在唐朝由盛转衰的历史时期，他目睹了唐朝上层社会的奢靡与社会危机，其诗多涉笔社会动荡、政治黑暗，他的诗反映了当时的社会矛盾和人民疾苦，记录了唐朝由盛转衰的历史巨变，表达了崇高的儒家仁爱精神和强烈的忧患意识。杜甫忧国忧民，人格高尚，诗艺精湛，其思想核心是仁政思想，其作品是现实主义诗歌的代表作。杜甫诗风沉郁顿挫，以古体、律诗见长，风格多样，代表作有《登高》《春望》《北征》《茅屋为秋风所破歌》等，对中国文学和日本文学都产生了深远的影响。

Du Fu

Du Fu (712-770), also known as Du Zimei, is a great realistic poet of the Tang Dynasty from Gongxian County (present-day Gongyi, Henan Province). He is known as the "Sage of Poetry," and his poems are believed to constitute a "history of poetry." About 1,500 of Du Fu's poems are extant today.

Living at a time when the Tang Dynasty was on the decline, Du Fu witnessed how extravagant and decadent the upper class was and how miserable the people were during the social crisis. His poems described social turmoil and political corruption, recorded the eventful period of Tang's fall, and reflected social conflicts and people's afflictions, expressing the Confucian spirit of benevolence and a strong sense of crisis.

Du Fu was a noble character who was deeply concerned about his country and people and a great poet whose works represent the realistic genre. His poems convey the central idea of benevolence underneath apparent gloominess and dismay. They are of diverse styles, and typical representatives include *On the Height*, *Spring View*, *To the North*, and *My Cottage Unroofed by Autumn Gales*. They have a far-reaching impact on Chinese and Japanese literature.

得中原者得天下

“得中原者得天下”这一古语意为得到中原这块地区的人，就可以得到天下。“逐鹿中原”“问鼎中原”等古语都阐明了一个道理，即河南省所在的中原地区，是中国几千年来的核心地区，执政并治理好中原，方可鼎立天下。

在古代，中原地区被视为政治、经济、文化和交通中心，是中国建都朝代最多、建都历史最长、古都数量最多的地区。在中国建都时间较长的八大古都中，河南省占据4个，包括洛阳、开封、安阳和郑州。河南地理位置优越，通往各地的交通都比较便利，大部分地区都处在华北平原上，土壤肥沃，是中国古代的重要粮仓。

在中华民族绵延不断的历史进程中，中原地区是华夏民族的摇篮，是中华民族产生、发展的核心区域，其深厚的文化积淀和悠久的文明为中华民族的茁壮成长提供了充足营养和不竭动力。中原地区由于独特的区位与文化优势，成为古代政治家、军事家争夺的战略要地，其治乱兴衰直接关系到

He Who Controls the Central Plains Will Control the Whole Country

There are a couple of idiomatic Chinese phrases expressing the idea that he who controls the Central Plains will control the whole country. This proves the important position of the Central Plains, where Henan Province is located, in China for thousands of years.

In ancient China, the Central Plains region was thought to be the political, economic, cultural and transportation center, boasting the largest number of capitals of the most dynasties for the longest history. Four of the eight major ancient capitals – Luoyang, Kaifeng, Anyang, and Zhengzhou – are located in Henan Province. In addition, with its favorable geographic position, convenient transportation to other places, and fertile land, Henan was an important breadbasket in ancient times.

The Central Plains region is the cradle of the Chinese nation. The profound cultural heritage and ancient civilization of the region have nourished and powered the birth, growth, and prosperity of the Chinese nation. Because of the unique geographical and cultural advantages, the Central Plains remained a strategic stronghold that ancient statesmen and military strategists had vied for, and the region's rise and fall, peace and chaos bore on the destiny of the entire country and nation. The saying that "he who controls the Central Plains will control the whole country"

整个国家和民族的命运。“得中原者得天下”就是反映了中原地区在国家政治和中华文明中无可替代的核心地位。

well demonstrates the irreplaceable core position of the region in state governance and the Chinese civilization.

走进河南篇

II

华夏古都

中国八大古代都城包括西安、洛阳、南京、北京、开封、杭州、安阳和郑州。其中，河南省占据四席，包括洛阳、开封、安阳、郑州。

洛阳拥有千年建都史，夏、商、西周、东周、东汉、三国魏、西晋、北魏、隋、唐（含武周）、后梁、后唐、后晋等十三朝以洛为都，洛阳成为中国建都时间最长的城市，拥有“十三朝古都”之称。

开封先后有夏朝、战国魏国、后梁、后晋、后汉、后周、宋朝、金朝等在此定都，有“八朝古都”之称，孕育了上承汉唐、下启明清、影响深远的“宋文化”。开封是世界上一座城市中轴线从未变动的都城，城摞城遗址在世界考古史和都城史上少有。

安阳是商朝的都城，甲骨文的故乡，后母戊鼎的发现

The Ancient Capital Cities

Among the eight major ancient capitals in China – Xi'an, Nanjing, Beijing, Hangzhou, Luoyang, Kaifeng, Anyang and Zhengzhou, the last four are all located in Henan Province.

Luoyang served as the capital of 13 dynasties and kingdoms for more than 1,000 years in total, the longest among all capital cities. The 13 dynasties are: Xia, Shang, Western Zhou, Eastern Zhou, Eastern Han, Kingdom of Wei during the Three Kingdoms Period, Western Jin, Northern Wei, Sui, Tang (including the Wuzhou era), Later Liang, Later Tang, and Later Jin.

Kaifeng served as the capital of eight ruling courts – Xia, State of Wei during the Warring States Period, Later Liang, Later Jin, Later Han, Later Zhou, Northern Song, and Jin. It nurtured the influential culture of the Song Dynasty, a transitioning period from the Han and the Tang to the Ming and the Qing dynasties. Throughout history, Kaifeng has had the same axis without any change, and the discovery of several capital cities underneath it, one on top of another, is a rarity in world archaeological history and the history of capitals.

Anyang first became a capital city more than 3,300 years ago and continued to serve as such for seven kingdoms or dynasties, including the Shang. It is the first

地，《周易》的发源地，也是中国历史上第一个文献可考并为甲骨文所证实的都城。安阳有着3300多年的建城史，前后共有七个王朝在安阳建都。

郑州有3000多年建都史，夏、商、西周管国、春秋郑国、战国韩国建都于此。郑州商城是迄今所知中国最早且规模最大的都城，也是中国历史上第一个建有城垣的王都。

capital city in Chinese history that is referenced in historical literature and corroborated by oracle-bone inscriptions. The oracle-bone inscriptions and the Houmuwu square cauldron were found here, and the book *Zhou Yi* was also created here.

Zhengzhou first became a capital city more than 3,000 years ago and served as such for the dynasties of Xia and Shang, State of Guan during the Western Zhou Dynasty, State of Zheng during the Spring and Autumn Period, and State of Han during the Warring States Period. The Shang Dynasty City Ruins in downtown Zhengzhou is the earliest and largest capital city discovered in China so far and the first capital protected by surrounding city walls.

安阳殷墟

殷墟，位于河南省安阳市，是中国商朝后期都城遗址，长宽各约6千米，总面积约36平方千米，遗产地保护区核心面积414公顷。殷墟的发掘是20世纪中国“100项重大考古发现”之首，确证了中国商王朝的存在，重构了中国古代早期历史的框架，使传统文献记载的商朝历史成为信史。

殷墟遗址主要包括殷墟王陵遗址、殷墟宫殿宗庙遗址、洹北商城遗址等，遗址中的宫殿宗庙区拥有80处房屋地基，还有唯一一座保存完好的商朝王室成员大墓“妇好墓”。殷墟出土的大量工艺精美的陪葬品证明了商朝手工业的先进水平。在王陵遗址东边出土的后母戊大方鼎，是迄今为止所发现的最重的青铜器。同时，在殷墟发现了大量甲骨窖穴。截至2022年11月，殷墟出土甲骨文大约有15万片。甲骨上的文字对于证明中国古代信仰、社会体系以及汉字的发展有着不可估量的价值。

Yin Xu in Anyang

The archaeological site of Yin Xu, located in Anyang of Henan Province, is the capital city of the late Shang Dynasty. The site covers an area about 6 kilometers in length and width each, and the core protected zone measures 414 hectares. The discovery of Yin Xu ranks first among China's top 100 major archaeological finds in the 20th century. It testifies to the existence of the Shang Dynasty and reframes the early history of ancient China, adding evidenced credibility to the Shang history recorded in ancient literature.

The Yin Xu site consists of a number of royal tombs, palaces, and ancestral shrines with about 80 house foundations, the Huanbei Shang City site, and the Tomb of Fu Hao, which is the only well-preserved tomb of a Shang royal member. The large number and superb craftsmanship of the burial accessories found at Yin Xu bear testimony to the advanced crafts industry at the time. The Houmuwu square cauldron unearthed in the east of the royal burial ground is the heaviest bronze vessel discovered so far. Large quantities of oracle bones – roughly 150,000 pieces as of November 2022 – have also been found at Yin Xu, and the inscriptions on them are invaluable proofs of the ancient beliefs and social systems of China and the development of its writing system.

殷墟代表了中国早期文化、工艺和科学的黄金时代，是中国青铜器时代最繁荣的时期。2006年7月，安阳殷墟被列入联合国教科文组织《世界遗产名录》，成为世界人民共同的文化遗产。

The Yin Xu site proves the existence of a golden age of early Chinese culture, crafts, and sciences, a time of great prosperity of the Chinese Bronze Age. In July 2006, it was included in the UNESCO's World Heritage List.

登封“天地之中”历史建筑群

登封“天地之中”历史建筑群，位于河南省登封市嵩山地区，该建筑群中的各建筑建成时间从汉朝至清朝，时间跨度达2000多年。

在中国古代传统的宇宙观中，中国是位居天地中央之国，而天地中心则在中原地区的登封，因而这里成为中国早期王朝建都之地和文化荟萃中心，并在中华文明起源和民族形成过程中起着主导作用。中国古代哲学思想三大流派“儒、释、道”都在这里建立了弘扬传播本流派文化的核心基地，此处也成为人们测天量地的中心。因此，登封汇聚和留存了大量珍贵的文化纪念建筑，其精华即登封“天地之中”历史建筑群。

这组建筑群包括周公测景台和观星台、嵩岳寺塔、太室阙和中岳庙、少室阙、启母阙、嵩阳书院、会善寺、少林寺

Historic Monuments of Dengfeng in "The Center of Heaven and Earth"

This set of historic structures are located near Mount Songshan in Dengfeng, Henan Province. The buildings were built across a period of more than 2,000 years from the Han to the Qing Dynasty.

In its traditional outlook on the universe, China, or "Zhongguo" in Chinese that literally means the "central state," was believed to be in the center of heaven and earth, with Dengfeng in the Central Plains as the central point. The place therefore became the best choice as the capital and cultural center of the early dynasties, playing a preeminent role in the emergence of the Chinese civilization and the formation of the Chinese nation.

The three mainstream schools of philosophical thinking in ancient China – Confucianism, Buddhism, and Daoism – all had preaching centers here. Dengfeng was also where people observed and measured heaven and earth. As a result, a large number of valuable cultural and commemorative buildings were built here, the essence of which was the historic monuments in "The Center of Heaven and Earth."

The complex comprises 11 ancient buildings at eight sites: Zhougong Sundial Platform and Astronomical Observatory, Songyue Temple Pagoda, Taishi Towers and Zhongyue Temple, Shaoshi Towers, Qimu Towers,

建筑群（常住院、塔林和初祖庵）等8处11项历史建筑。历经汉、魏、唐、宋、元、明、清，绵延不绝，构成了一部中国中原地区上下2000年形象直观的建筑史。

“天地之中”历史建筑群有着广泛的国际影响，其中，少林寺更是举世闻名。少林寺始建于公元495年，是中国佛教禅宗祖庭和中国功夫的发源地之一，被誉为“天下第一名刹”，在世界佛教史中具有重要地位。2010年8月，登封“天地之中”历史建筑群被列入联合国教科文组织《世界遗产名录》。

Songyang Academy, Huishan Temple, and Shaolin Temple compounds (resident compounds, Pagoda Forest and Chuzu Temple). Standing through 2,000 years from the Han, Wei, Tang, Song, and Yuan all the way to the Ming and Qing dynasties, it is in itself a living history book of architecture in the Central Plains.

The historic monuments of Dengfeng, especially the Shaolin Temple, are world-renowned. First built in 495, the Shaolin Temple is the cradle of the Chan sect of Chinese Buddhism and a birthplace of Chinese *kung fu*. It is reputed as the "No. 1 temple in the world" for its pivotal position in world Buddhist history. In August 2010, these historic buildings were included in the UNESCO's World Heritage List.

“中华第一龙”

“中华第一龙”是指在河南省濮阳市一处早期仰韶文化遗址中发现的蚌壳龙形图案，此龙昂首、曲颈、弓身、长尾，前爪扒、后爪蹬，状似腾飞。经中国社会科学院考古研究所测定，蚌龙的年代约为公元前4600年，遂被称为“中华第一龙”。

中国是龙的故乡，“中华第一龙”的发现不仅为中国的龙形象找到了源头，而且在龙文化研究上有多方面的重要意义。龙文化源远流长，是中国文化的突出符号。中国历代正史记载的龙事件大概有三百多起，其他类型的文献更是丰富。龙文化深入到了中国社会的各个角落，影响波及了文化的各个层面。龙装饰、龙雕刻、舞龙、二月二龙抬头、龙须面、龙舟赛等，都是几千年来流行于民间的龙文化。

龙作为中华民族的象征，数千年来已深深扎根于中国人的心中，形成了具有强大凝聚力的龙文化。对现代中国人来说，龙的形象是一种符号、一种血肉相联的情感，“龙的子

No. 1 Dragon in China

This refers to the dragon-shaped pattern laid out with clamshells at an early Yangshao Culture site in Puyang, Henan Province. The dragon has a raised head, a curvy neck, an arched body, and a long tail, and it looks ready to soar with its front and rear claws pushing the ground. The Institute of Archaeology under the Chinese Academy of Social Sciences dated the clamshell dragon at around 4600 BC, hence the name the "No. 1 dragon in China."

Dragons play an important role in the Chinese culture. In addition to unveiling the origin of the dragon image in China, the discovery of the clamshell dragon has multifold significance for the study of the long-standing dragon culture, which is a prominent token of the Chinese culture. Official historical documents have recorded more than 300 dragon-related events, not to mention numerous records in other forms. The dragon culture, having enjoyed wide popularity for thousands of years, is embedded in every aspect of Chinese society and culture, as manifested in such forms as dragon-themed adornments, carvings, dances, festivals, noodles, and boating races.

Dragon, as a symbol of the Chinese nation, has evolved into a culture that holds the Chinese people together. For modern Chinese, it stands for a bond of flesh and blood, and terms like "offspring of the dragon" and "descendants of the

孙”“龙的传人”这些称谓，令中国人激动、奋发、自豪。龙的文化除在中华大地上传播和承继外，还被海外华人广泛传播，增进了世界各国人民对中华文化的了解和认同。

dragon" fill them with aspiration and pride. Not only being inherited and promoted at home, the dragon culture is also widely spread by overseas Chinese, helping the rest of the world better understand China and its culture.

洛阳龙门石窟

龙门石窟位于河南省洛阳市，是世界上现存造像数量最多、规模最大的石刻艺术宝库，与敦煌莫高窟、云冈石窟和麦积山石窟并称为中国四大石窟，并位居四大石窟之首。

龙门石窟始凿于北魏时期，盛于唐，终于清末，历经10多个朝代营造长达1400余年，是世界上营造时间最长的石窟。建造时采用了大量彩绘，今多已褪色。龙门石窟密布于伊水东西两山的峭壁上，南北长达1千米，现存洞窟像龛2345个，造像11万余尊。龙门石窟造像多为皇家贵族所建，是世界上绝无仅有的皇家石窟。

龙门石窟规模宏大，气势磅礴，窟内造像雕刻精湛，内容题材丰富，有大量宗教、美术、建筑、书法、音乐、服饰、医药等方面的实物资料，从不同侧面反映了中国古代政

Longmen Grottoes in Luoyang

The Longmen Grottoes located in Luoyang, Henan Province are a treasure house of stone carvings, boasting the largest number and scale of stone statues. The site ranks top of the four major grottoes in China, followed by the Mogao Grottoes in Dunhuang of Gansu Province, the Yungang Grottoes in Datong of Shanxi Province, and the Maiji Mountain Grottoes in Tianshui of Gansu Province.

The carving of the Longmen Grottoes began in the Northern Wei Dynasty (386-534), came into full swing in the Tang Dynasty, and was completed in the late Qing Dynasty, spanning more than 1,400 years through over 10 dynasties, the longest in the world. The grottoes contained colored paintings, though mostly faded today. Densely located on both banks of the Yishui River, the Longmen Grottoes comprise more than 110,000 stone statues shrined in 2,345 caves and niches carved into the steep cliffs over a one-kilometer-long stretch from north to south. They are the only royal grottoes in the world as most of the statues were built under the patronage of the royal families.

The magnificent Longmen Grottoes, the exquisite statues in the caves, and the wide variety of themes and contents make a valuable, comprehensive library of materials and references regarding religion, art, architecture, calligraphy, music, apparel, medicine, and other aspects.

治、经济、宗教、文化等许多领域的发展变化，为中国石窟艺术的创新与发展作出了重大贡献。

龙门石窟还涵盖诸多域外元素，例如西域乐器、古希腊石柱、欧洲纹样等，这些都彰显了龙门石窟是多元文明交融的产物。龙门石窟不仅展现了中国历史悠久的艺术形式，也为推动世界文化多样性发挥了重要作用。2000年11月，龙门石窟被列入联合国教科文组织《世界遗产名录》。

They reflect from different perspectives the evolution in ancient China's politics, economy, religions, culture, and other sectors and make great contributions to the innovation and development of Chinese grotto art.

The Longmen Grottoes also abound in exotic elements, such as musical instruments from the Western Regions, ancient Greek columns, and European emblazonry, indicating the blending and fusion of various civilizations back in the years. They not only display China's time-honored art forms, but also preserve world cultural diversity. In November 2000, they were included in the UNESCO's World Heritage List.

洛阳白马寺

白马寺位于河南省洛阳市，始建于东汉时期，是佛教传入中国后兴建的第一座官办寺院，占地约4万平方米，有大小建筑百余间。最早传入中国的梵文佛经《贝叶经》收藏于白马寺，最早的译经道场在白马寺的清凉台，第一本汉文佛经《四十二章经》在白马寺译出，第一位汉族僧人朱士行受戒于白马寺。因此，白马寺被尊称为“祖庭”“释源”，即祖师之庭院、佛教之发源。

据记载，公元64年，汉明帝遣特使赴天竺求佛法，途中他们遇到印度高僧摄摩腾和竺法兰，便请二位高僧东赴中国弘法布教。一行人用白马驮载佛经、佛像回到国都洛阳之后，汉明帝敕令在洛阳兴建僧院，为纪念白马驮经，取名“白马寺”。之后，又有多位西方高僧来到白马寺译经，这里

Baima Temple in Luoyang

The Baima Temple, or White Horse Temple, in Luoyang was the first government-funded temple built after Buddhism was introduced into China in the Eastern Han Dynasty. The temple once housed the earliest Sanskrit Buddhist scripture introduced to China, which was written on pattra leaves, and its Clear Cool Terrace served as the earliest scripture translation workshop. It is also where the *Sutra of Forty-Two Chapters* was translated into Chinese, the first Chinese version of a Buddhist scripture, and where the first Han monk, Zhu Shixing, was initiated into Buddhism. This is why the temple is honored as the ancestral temple and the place of origin of Chinese Buddhism.

It is recorded that Emperor Ming of the Eastern Han Dynasty assigned special envoys in AD 64 to India in search of Buddhist scriptures. On their way, the envoys came across two eminent Indian monks, Kāśyapamātaṅga and Dharmaratna, and invited them to China to preach Buddhism. The team returned to Luoyang, the capital then, with white horses carrying Buddhist sutras and statues on their backs, so the emperor had a temple built and named it Baima Temple in honor of the accomplishment. Later, a couple of other eminent monks from the Western Regions came to the temple and translated Buddhist scriptures here,

成为当之无愧的中国"第一译经道场"。佛教由此传播到朝鲜、日本和东南亚，在亚洲得到普及，后来又进入欧美，白马寺因此成为世界各地佛教信徒参拜的圣地。

20世纪末以来，泰国、印度和缅甸政府相继出资在白马寺建造佛殿，使之成为全世界唯一拥有中、印、缅、泰四国风格佛殿的国际化寺院。

making it the well-deserved "first scripture translation workshop" in China. It was from here that Buddhism spread to the Korean Peninsular, Japan, and Southeast Asia and further to Europe and America, and the Baima Temple therefore became a place worshipped by Buddhists around the world.

Since the end of the 20th century, the governments of Thailand, India, and Myanmar have successively built Buddhist halls at the Baima Temple, turning it into the world's only international temple embracing the styles of China and the three countries.

洛阳牡丹甲天下

中国名花洛阳牡丹，是中国国家地理标志产品，栽培始于隋，鼎盛于唐，宋时甲于天下，至今已有1400多年的历史。洛阳牡丹花朵硕大，品种繁多，花色奇绝，有红、白、粉、黄、紫、蓝、绿、黑及复色9大色系、10种花型、1400多个品种，素有“国色天香”“花中之王”的美称，长期以来被当作富贵吉祥、繁荣兴旺的象征。

“洛阳牡丹甲天下”，这是千百年来人们对洛阳牡丹的赞誉，故洛阳有“千年帝都，牡丹花城”之称。洛阳早在唐宋时期即已具备系统的栽花技艺，形成赏花习俗及与牡丹有关的诗词、书画、传说、服饰等，由此衍生出洛阳牡丹文化，这也是河洛文化的重要组成部分。牡丹不仅具有观赏价值，其花、种、根、粉都有着很高的经济价值，已开发出中药、食品、酿酒、化妆品、保健茶等系列产品。

1983年以来，洛阳市在每年四五月举办牡丹花会。2019年5月，在北京世园会牡丹芍药国际竞赛中，洛阳牡丹

Luoyang Peony, Queen of Flowers

The Luoyang peony is a Geographical Indication product in China. First cultivated in the Sui Dynasty (581-618) more than 1,400 years ago, the flower had its heyday in the Tang Dynasty and became the best-known garden plant in the Song Dynasty (960-1279). The Luoyang peony features a large size, and there are more than 1,400 varieties, 10 flower shapes, and 9 color systems (red, white, pink, yellow, purple, blue, green, black, and multicolor). Hailed as the "queen of flowers," it has long been favored as a symbol of wealth, good luck, and prosperity.

For over a thousand years, Luoyang has been reputed to be the "city of peony." As early as in the Tang and the Song dynasties, advanced floriculture, the custom of flower appreciation, and peony-related poetry, calligraphy, painting, legends, and garments had already appeared in Luoyang, and the peony culture stemming from these is an important part of the Heluo culture. In addition to pleasing the eyes, peony is of high economic value as its petals, seeds, roots, and pollen can all be used to make medicine, food, wine, cosmetics, and tonic tea.

A Peony Fair has been held in Luoyang every spring in April and May since 1983. At the International Peony Competition held in May 2019 during the International Horticultural Exhibition in Beijing, the Luoyang peony

共获奖项221个，获奖总数及各类奖项均列所有参赛团体第一，再次印证了“洛阳牡丹甲天下”的美誉。

won 221 awards, ranking first of all candidates in terms of the total number of awards and the respective numbers of awards in different categories, once again corroborating its unrivaled reputation.

大运河河南段

大运河是以人工河道为主形成的国家核心水道网络体系，特指中国各朝代传承的南北运河网络体系。历史上各阶段的大运河可以冠以朝代的名称，如秦汉大运河、隋唐大运河、明清大运河等。隋唐大运河以洛阳为中心，以通济渠、永济渠为“人”字状两大撇捺延伸，沟通了海河、黄河、淮河、长江、钱塘江五大水系，长达3000千米，北通涿郡（今北京），南达余杭（今杭州），建成了以西安和洛阳为核心的全国性高等级水路运输通道，被认为是大运河发展史上最重要的标志。

河南省境内的大运河遗址主要分布在洛阳、郑州、开封、商丘、焦作、新乡、鹤壁、安阳和濮阳9个城市。从隋唐至宋元长达700多年的时间里，河南一直是大运河的中心。在历史上，大运河河南段充分发挥了政治、经济、社会作用，其通过水道连接南北，大大加强了中国南北的沟通；

Henan Sections of the Grand Canal

The Grand Canal is a national network of artificial waterways that specifically refers to the north-south canal system constructed through several dynasties in China. The sections dug in different historical periods are usually named after the dynasties, such as the Qin-Han Grand Canal, the Sui-Tang Grand Canal, and the Ming-Qing Grand Canal.

At the center of the Sui-Tang Grand Canal is Luoyang, from which the waterway runs in a herringbone shape, with the Yongji Canal running northward to Zhuojun (present-day Beijing) and the Tongji Canal southward to Yuhang (present-day Hangzhou). The Sui-Tang Grand Canal thus extends 3,000 kilometers and connects the five water systems – Haihe, Yellow, Huaihe, Yangtze, and Qiantang. It forms a national high-level water route centered on Luoyang and is considered the most important milestone in the history of the Grand Canal.

The Grand Canal sites within Henan Province are located in nine cities – Luoyang, Zhengzhou, Kaifeng, Shangqiu, Jiaozuo, Xinxiang, Hebi, Anyang, and Puyang. For a period of more than 700 years from the Sui and the Tang to the Song and the Yuan dynasties, Henan remained the center of the Grand Canal. The local sections had played an important political, economic and social role by strengthening the connection and communication between

同时也促进了洛阳、开封、郑州、商丘等城市的发展，推动了中原城市经济的繁荣。

当前，大运河河南段正进一步开发运河沿线的自然景观资源、生态系统资源、古建筑资源以及人文资源。2014年6月，联合国教科文组织将中国大运河列入《世界遗产名录》。

northern and southern China, promoting the development of Luoyang, Kaifeng, Zhengzhou, and Shangqiu, and invigorating the economy in the Central Plains.

Today, great efforts have been made to preserve the natural landscape ecosystem, ancient buildings, and cultural resources along the Henan sections. In June 2014, the Grand Canal was included in the UNESCO's World Heritage List.

丝绸之路河南段崤函古道

丝绸之路是西汉时期开辟的中国通往中亚、西亚、地中海各国的陆上通道。它最初的作用是运输丝绸，在明朝时期成为综合贸易之路。

丝绸之路河南段崤函古道是陕西潼关至河南省新安县、宜阳县之间的一段古代丝绸之路遗址，其主体部分位于河南省三门峡市。据古书记载，崤函古道有东西两段，在今三门峡境内，就长达400华里（200千米）。

崤函古道中的“崤”和“函”分别指古崤山和函谷关。崤函古道是丝绸之路上的锁钥要塞。一方面，其独特的地理地貌形成了一条天然的交通通道，成为古代中原地区通往关中地区的要道，战略意义重大。另一方面，其东端是河洛平原，西端是关中平原，北面是晋南平原。这个地区是中华文明发源的核心地区。

在世界史上，丝绸之路崤函古道是中原通往西域的唯一通道，推动了中原与西域、亚欧的经贸往来与人文交流。

Xiaohan Ancient Path of the Silk Road

The Silk Road is a land route opened in the Western Han Dynasty (206 BC-AD 24) to link China with Central Asia, West Asia, and the Mediterranean area. Initially serving to transport silk, the Silk Road became a busy trade route in the Ming Dynasty.

The Xiaohan Ancient Path is the Henan section of the Silk Road. The "Xiao" refers to the Xiaoshan Mountain and the "Han," the Hangu Pass. Through the deep valley between them there is a narrow passage that stretches from Xin'an and Yiyang counties of Henan Province in the east to the Tongguan Pass of Shaanxi Province in the west, with the main part running through Sanmenxia of Henan for about 200 kilometers.

The Xiaohan Ancient Path was a vital passage on the Silk Road. Given the unique geography, this natural strategic traffic route connected the Central Plains in the east with the Guanzhong region in the west. With the Heluo Plain in the east, the Guanzhong Plain in the west, and the Jinnan Plain in the north, the area nearby was at the very center of the origin of the Chinese civilization.

The Xiaohan Path was once the only route for the Central Plains people to travel to the Western Regions, which thus significantly boosted the economic, trade and cultural ties between Asia and Europe. In June 2014,

2014年6月，联合国教科文组织正式将包括崤函古道在内的丝绸之路列入“世界遗产名录”。

the Silk Road, including the Xiaohan Ancient Path, was included in the UNESCO's World Heritage List.

云台山世界地质公园

云台山位于河南省焦作市，总面积280平方千米，是一处以太行山岳水景为特色，以峡谷类地质地貌景观和历史文化为内涵，集科学价值和美学价值于一身的自然景观与地质公园。

云台山因山势险峻，峰壑之间常年云锁雾绕而得名。云台山风景区含红石峡、潭瀑峡、泉瀑峡、子房湖、茱萸峰、叠彩洞、猕猴谷、百家岩、万善寺等主要景点。主峰茱萸峰海拔约1300米；坐落在泉瀑峡内的云台天瀑单级落差314米，是亚洲单级落差最大的瀑布，被誉为“华夏第一高瀑”，是云台山标志性景观之一。

云台山地质遗迹丰富，现已发现34亿年前的岩层。30多亿年来，形成了太古宇、元古宇、古生界和新生界地层，尤其是2300万年以来，新构造运动的强烈抬升和水蚀作用的深度下切，造就了云台山双崖对峙的峡谷群和各种动态的瀑、泉、溪、潭，共同构成了“云台地貌”景观。

在中国历史上，云台山不仅受到了诸多帝王将相、文人

Yuntaishan Global Geopark

Yuntaishan, or the Yuntai Mountain, is located in Jiaozuo, Henan Province. The geopark is distinguished by its majestic mountain view and captivating waterscape. It presents awe-inspiring canyon geology and landform and embodies a rich historical and cultural heritage, integrating great scientific and aesthetic value.

The mountain got its name "Yuntai" (literally meaning "cloud platform") from the perennial clouds lingering among its steep peaks and valleys. The Yuntai Mountain Scenic Area boasts appealing views of valleys, lakes, peaks, caves, and temples. The summit of Zhuyu Peak erects 1,300 meters above the sea level. The Yuntai Sky Waterfall, the landmark waterfall with a single drop of 314 meters, is the highest of its kind in Asia.

The Yuntai Mountain is home to rich geological relics, including rock strata dating back 3.4 billion years as well as the Archean, Proterozoic, Paleozoic and Cenozoic strata. In particular, the neotectonics and water erosion over the last 23 million years have created the fabulous clusters of valleys sandwiched between steep cliffs and a variety of cascades, springs, streams, and ponds. All these constitute the unique Yuntai landform.

While being favored by the emperors, high-rank officials, and the literati in history, the Yuntai Mountain

雅士的青睐，而且佛教和道教也在此相互影响，使之成为一座底蕴厚重的宗教名山。2004年2月，云台山被联合国教科文组织评选为全球首批世界地质公园。

also has a profound religious legacy left through the mutual influence between Buddhism and Daoism. In February 2004, it was designated by the UNESCO as one of the first global geoparks.

少林功夫

少林功夫发源于河南省登封市嵩山少林寺，是中国历史文化遗产——中华武术的重要组成部分，是中国武术界各大流派中历史最悠久、种类最繁多、体系最庞大、最具文化内涵的门派。

少林功夫早期形式多是实战的格斗技法，在发展中吸收各家流派之长，将少林功夫套路归纳成完备的武术体系。明朝万历年间，少林寺把禅修引入医疗之中，形成独具特色的少林医术，从而把禅宗、武术和医学融为一体，形成以“以禅修心、以武健体、以医养身”为核心的少林禅武医文化，即“少林三宝”。1500多年来，少林功夫有序传承、从未间断，由最初保护寺院、强身健体的手段，逐渐发展成为技术完备、内涵丰富的文化表现形式。

儒释道思想对于少林功夫的精神价值取向、思想伦理文化以及对外传播有着重要影响。儒家的“仁爱”观念奠定了武术的伦理道德和人文精神基础，把本来属于“暴力”行为

Shaolin *Kung Fu*

The Shaolin *kung fu* originated in the Shaolin Temple on Mount Songshan in Dengfeng, Henan Province. It is an important sect of the Chinese martial arts, boasting the longest history, greatest diversity, widest range, and most profound cultural significance of all martial arts schools.

Mostly about real-combat fighting in its early stage, the Shaolin *kung fu* has evolved into a well-developed system by drawing upon the strengths of other schools and blending them with its own routines. From 1573 to 1620 in the Ming Dynasty, the monks of the Shaolin Temple introduced the Buddhist practice of meditation into medical treatment, thus integrating the Chan Buddhism (cultivating the heart), martial arts (enhancing physical fitness), and medicine (caring for the body) into a unique trio known as the "three treasures of Shaolin." For more than 1,500 years, the Shaolin *kung fu* has been passed down consistently without interruption, evolving from a means of defending the temple and improving physical health into a systematic cultural form with a whole set of techniques and rich connotations.

Confucianism, Buddhism, and Daoism all have major influence on the values, ethics, and dissemination of the Shaolin *kung fu*. The Confucian concept of benevolence, as the moral and cultural basis of martial arts, transforms the originally "violent" fighting into something that could

的武术纳入到正统思想规范中；道家的“道法自然”理念，使习练者追求人与自然的和谐相通，使武术技能服从自然的变化规律，求得“物我”“内外”的平衡；二者与佛教理念相结合，成为少林功夫形成与发展的重要因素，保障了其稳定发展和普及。2006年，少林功夫入选中国国家级非物质文化遗产保护名录。

如今，少林功夫在海内外广泛传播，发展成为流传广泛、影响深远的武术流派，拥有“天下功夫出少林”之称，成为中国功夫的代名词。

be incorporated into the mainstream norms. The Daoist idea of "letting things take their natural course" prompts the practitioners to pursue harmony between man and nature and adapt martial arts skills to the changes of nature till a balance can be achieved between the object and the self and between the inner and the outer worlds. These two teachings, combined with the Buddhist philosophy, bear heavily on the formation and development of the Shaolin *kung fu* by guaranteeing its steady evolution and popularization. In 2006, the Shaolin *kung fu* was included in China's list of national intangible cultural heritage.

Nowadays, the Shaolin *kung fu* is widely spread across the world as a martial arts school of extensive and deep-going influence. It has become the epitome of the Chinese martial arts, as expressed in the saying that "all martial arts under heaven originated from Shaolin."

太极拳

太极拳是以中国传统文化中的儒、释、道、武、医等思想为理论基础，以太极阴阳哲理为健身和技击技术应用的指导思想而发展起来的一种中国传统武术。太极拳的创始起源尚未有定论，一说起源于河南省焦作市陈家沟村。

太极拳综合历代各家拳法，形成了含蓄内敛、连绵不断、以柔克刚、急缓相间、行云流水的拳术风格。习练者用意念统领全身，通过反复习练，进入意、气、形、神趋于圆融一体的至高境界，达到修身养性、陶冶情操、强身健体、益寿延年的目的。

太极拳所蕴含的“阴阳循环”“天人合一”的中国传统哲学思想和养生观念，丰富了人们对宇宙、自然和人体运行规律的认知；“尊师重道”“学拳不可狂、不可满”等价值观念，潜移默化地涵养着人们平和、包容、友善的心性，在促

Taijiquan

Taijiquan, also known as *tai chi chuan* or *tai chi*, is a set of traditional Chinese martial arts that has its theoretical roots in Confucianism, Buddhism, Daoism, and ancient ideas about exercise and medicine. Its exercising and attacking techniques are practiced following the *taiji* and *yin-yang* theories. There is no conclusion about the origin of *Taijiquan* yet, but some argue that it was created in Chenjiagou Village in Jiaozhuo, Henan Province.

A combination of elements of various boxing schools, *Taijiquan* is known for its reserved and flowing style that emphasizes overcoming the hard with the soft and balancing the swift with the slow. Practitioners control their whole body with the will and keep practicing till reaching an ultimate realm of unity of the will, *qi* (an internal force or power), body, and mind, thus achieving physical, mental and moral advancement.

The philosophical concepts and regimen contained in *Taijiquan*, such as the "cycle of *yin* and *yang*" and "man is an integral part of nature," enrich people's perception of the universe, nature, and the way that the human body works. The values such as "respecting the teacher and moral norms" and "boxing practitioners should never be arrogant and conceited" make people peaceful, inclusive, and kind. *Taijiquan* plays an important role in promoting

进身心健康、推动人与人和谐共处、增强社会凝聚力等方面发挥着重要作用。

目前，太极拳已传播到150多个国家和地区，习练者达三亿多人，是世界上参与人数最多、最受人们喜爱的武术运动和健身活动之一，成为促进中外文化交流的重要纽带。2020年12月，太极拳被列入联合国教科文组织“人类非物质文化遗产代表作名录”。

people's physical and mental health, fostering harmonious interpersonal relations, and enhancing social cohesion.

Taijiquan is now practiced by over 300 million people in more than 150 countries and regions. It is one of the forms of martial arts and fitness activities with the most followers and greatest popularity and has become a bond of cultural exchanges between China and the rest of the world. In December 2020, it was inscribed on the UNESCO's Representative List of the Intangible Cultural Heritage of Humanity.

《清明上河图》

中国十大传世名画之一《清明上河图》是中国古典现实主义绘画的杰作，由北宋著名画家张择端创作，描绘了北宋宣和年间（1119—1125）都城的繁华景象，为国宝级文物，现藏于北京故宫博物院。

清明上河是当时的民间风俗，类似于今天的节日集会。《清明上河图》生动记录了12世纪北宋都城东京（今河南省开封市）的城市面貌和当时社会各阶层人民的生活状况，是北宋时期繁荣发达的历史见证，也是北宋城市经济情况的生动写照。

《清明上河图》采用全景式构图，以自然景观作为分隔，展示了郊野、汴河、街市三部分景象。作者采用了大手笔与精细手笔相结合的技法，使得画卷内容丰富、生动有趣、紧凑而精细。在长528.7厘米、宽24.8厘米的长卷中，作者共绘就了数量庞大的各色人物，牛、骡、驴等牲畜，车、轿、船等交通工具，房屋、桥梁、城楼等建筑。画卷结

Qing Ming Shang He Tu

Qing Ming Shang He Tu (*A Riverside Scene on the Qingming Festival*) is a masterpiece of classical, realistic painting and one of the 10 most distinguished paintings left from ancient China. Painted by Zhang Zeduan, a court painter of the Northern Song Dynasty, it captures the bustling capital city in the Xuanhe reign period (1119-1125). The painting, a national treasure now, is housed in the Palace Museum in Beijing.

Gathering by the riverside on the Qingming (Pure Brightness) Festival was a folk custom back then, resembling the festive fair in modern times. The painting vividly depicts what Dongjing (present-day Kaifeng, Henan Province), capital city of the Northern Song, was like and how the people of various classes lived in the 12th century, bearing perpetual witness to the dynasty's economic prosperity.

With a panoramic composition, the painting gives a lively view of the outskirts, the Bianhe River, and the streets of Dongjing, which are separated ingeniously by natural landscapes. Outlined with both magnificence and exquisiteness, the work provides a wealth of contents in a compact and delicate way. The 528.7-centimeter-long, 24.8-centimeter-wide scroll presents, in meticulous delineation, all kinds of people, animals (e.g. cattle, mules,

构严谨、段落分明，画中各类人物、景物、货物细节井然有序。这在中国乃至世界绘画史上都是独一无二的。

《清明上河图》不仅是一件伟大的现实主义绘画艺术珍品，同时也提供了北宋大都市的商业、手工业、民俗、建筑等详实形象的第一手资料，具有重要的艺术价值和历史文献价值。其丰富的思想内涵、独特的审美视角、现实主义的表现手法，使其在中国乃至世界绘画史上均被奉为经典之作。

and donkeys), traffic tools (e.g. carts, sedans, and boats), and buildings (e.g. houses, bridges, and city towers). It is one-of-a-kind in China's and the world's painting history for its rigorous composition, clear-cut sections, and carefully rendered details of various characters, landscapes, and goods.

The painting has both artistic and historical significance for its realistic reflection of the capital city and presentation of first-hand materials on the commerce, craft, folklore, and architecture of a metropolitan in the Song Dynasty. Its rich cultural connotations, unique aesthetic, and realistic expressions make it a classic masterpiece of all times.

商丘火神台庙会

商丘火神台坐落在河南省商丘市睢阳区古城西南2千米处，是人们为纪念火神阏伯而建。公元前2300年，阏伯发明了以火纪时的历法，在管火的同时筑造阏伯台观察星辰，据此测定自然变化和年成好坏，为古代中国的天文学作出了重要贡献。阏伯呕心沥血、教化民众，深受人民爱戴，被民间尊为“火神”。

传说农历正月初七是阏伯的诞辰，自古以来，商丘周边豫、鲁、苏、皖四省交界的群众，特别是商汤子姓的后裔子孙，在这一天前后，怀着对祖先无比崇敬的心情，前去朝台进香，于是形成规模盛大的庙会。庙会一般从农历正月初一开始，到二月二方散。六月二十三，也是传说中火神的祭

Huoshentai Temple Fair in Shangqiu

Huoshentai (God of Fire Platform), located about two kilometers to the southwest of the ancient city site of Shangqiu, Henan Province, was built in memory of Yan Bo, the God of Fire and the earliest ancestor of the Shang clan. In 2300 BC, Yan Bo invented a calendar that marked time based on the movement of Antares, called the "star of fire" by the ancient people, and built a platform to observe the stars to predict natural changes and harvest, making great contributions to astronomy in ancient China. Yan Bo devoted himself to teaching and helping the people and was deeply loved by them and remembered as the "God of Fire."

Legend has it that the seventh day of the first month in the lunar calendar is the birthday of Yan Bo. Since ancient times, the local residents and people living in the neighboring provinces of Shandong, Jiangsu, and Anhui, especially those with surnames originating from "Zi," the surname of Tang who was the first ruler of the Shang Dynasty, would visit the star-observing platform around this day and burn incense sticks to commemorate their ancestor. This activity has gradually evolved into a grand temple fair that usually lasts a month – from the first day of the first month to the second day of the second month in the lunar calendar. There is also another fair, lasting about 10 days around the 23rd day of the sixth lunar month, the alleged

日，周边四省群众仍是络绎不绝，朝台进香，庙会一般也长达10天。

火神台庙会以商丘悠久的历史文化资源为依托，以火神台景区为平台，以火神祭祀为载体，整合利用商丘丰富的群众文化元素及民间民俗文化资源，将商丘地区独具特色的民俗民间文化资源荟萃于此，打造成了具有浓郁豫东特色的民俗活动盛典。2021年5月，商丘火神台庙会被列入国家级非物质文化遗产名录。

anniversary of the death of the God of Fire, when people would come to the platform again to worship the god.

The Huoshentai Temple Fair, deriving from Shangqiu's long history and traditional culture and incorporating its rich, distinct folk customs, has become a public gala infused with strong eastern Henan charatcteristics. A scenic zone is also developed around the platform. In May 2021, the Shangqiu Huoshentai Temple Fair was included in China's list of national intangible cultural heritage.

重阳节

重阳节是中国传统节日，相传起源于河南省上蔡县，节期在农历九月初九。“九”在《易经》中为阳数（奇数），“九九”为两阳数相重，故曰“重阳”。古人认为，九九重阳是吉祥的日子。

据现存史料考证，重阳节源自天象崇拜，起始于上古，普及于西汉，鼎盛于唐朝以后。上古时代人们在秋季举行丰收祭天、祭祖活动，以谢天帝、祖先恩德，这是重阳节的原始形式。在历史发展演变中，重阳节融合多种民俗为一体，承载了更为丰富的文化内涵。传承至今，又添加了敬老等内涵。中国将每年农历九月初九定为敬老日，使这一传统佳节成为尊老、敬老、爱老、助老的新式节日。

九九重阳凝聚了中华民族“老吾老”的浓浓深情和生生不息的民族风范，以富有生命意蕴的节庆活动世代流传，设宴敬老、饮宴祈寿主题逐渐和中国传统孝道伦理相融合，成为当今重阳节节庆活动的重要主题。2006年5月，重阳节被列入首批国家级非物质文化遗产名录。

Chongyang Festival

The Chongyang Festival is a traditional Chinese festival allegedly originating in Shangcai County of Henan Province. It falls on the ninth day of the ninth month in the lunar calendar, so it is also known as the Double Ninth Festival, a date that the ancient people held to be auspicious.

According to historical materials, the Chongyang Festival had its initial form in the ceremonies held in autumn to worship heaven and the ancestors in gratitude for the harvest. It prevailed in the Western Han Dynasty and reached its peak in the Tang Dynasty. As time goes by, the festival has absorbed various folk customs and assumed richer cultural significance, including the more recently added respecting and caring for the elderly as China in 1989 designated this traditional festival the Senior Citizens Day.

The Chongyang Festival embodies the Chinese nation's virtue of loving the seniors. In modern times, its celebrations are usually themed on health and longevity mixed with the traditional ethics of filial piety. In May 2006, the festival was among the first inscribed on the list of national intangible cultural heritage.

豫剧

豫剧是发源于河南省、流传于全国各地的传统戏剧，因为其音乐伴奏用枣木梆子打拍，故又名“河南梆子”，已有上百年的传承历史，与京剧、越剧、评剧、黄梅戏并称为“中国五大戏曲剧种”。

豫剧早在清朝乾隆年间就已成为中国极具影响力的戏曲剧种之一。豫剧在生成和发展时期，汲取了多种戏曲剧种的艺术因素，广泛吸收河南民间流行的音乐、曲艺说唱和俗曲小令，形成了朴直淳厚、丰富细腻、富于乡土气息的剧种特色。

豫剧艺术长期受中原文化特别是黄河流域地域文化影响，在演出剧目、舞台表演、人物塑造、表述方式、音乐唱腔等方面形成了独特的河南地方风格，唱腔铿锵大气、抑扬有度，行腔酣畅、吐字清晰，善于表达人物内心情感，散发着无穷的艺术魅力，是中国戏曲宝库中的珍贵财富。豫剧在剧目生产、剧团数量、观众人数、市场效益等方面，为当代地方戏之翘楚。2006年5月，豫剧被列入第一批国家级非物质文化遗产名录。

Yuju Opera

Yuju, or Henan Opera, is a traditional opera originating in Henan Province with wide popularity. It is also called Henan *bangzi* because the performance is accompanied with *bangzi* ("clappers") made of jujube wood. With a history of more than 100 years, it is one of the five major opera schools in China together with Peking Opera, Yueju Opera, Pingju Opera, and Huangmei Opera.

Yuju Opera was a highly influential genre during Emperor Qianlong's reign (1736-1795) in the Qing Dynasty. As it developed, it took in the elements of many other opera schools and extensively absorbed the folk music, singing art, and short lyrics popular in Henan, growing into a distinct local opera featuring straightforward plain expressions, a rich variety of topics and contents, and fine and nuanced sentiments.

Immersed in the Central Plains culture, especially the Yellow River culture, the opera gives off a unique Henan style in its repertoire, performance, characterization, expression, and melody. Unconstrained, cadent, and articulate, this enchantingly expressive art form makes a valuable asset and a crown jewel in China's large pool of local operas for its large number of troupes and programs, vast audience base, and great economic benefits. In May 2006, Yuju Opera was placed on China's first list of national intangible cultural heritage.

《唐宫夜宴》

《唐宫夜宴》是2021年河南卫视春节联欢晚会播出的女子群舞剧，讲述唐朝时期一群少女准备赴宴表演及夜宴演奏过程中的趣事。《唐宫夜宴》的创作灵感来源于河南博物院所藏隋代乐舞俑。在作品中，舞蹈演员身着唐三彩色样服装，脸上画着斜红妆容，仿佛博物院中的乐舞俑有了生命。该作品将中原文化之美展现得淋漓尽致，5G、AR技术将虚拟场景和现实舞台相融合，呈现出一场震撼人心的视觉盛宴。伴随着灵动的舞姿，古画和文物在现代科技舞美的辅助下，徐徐映入观众眼帘——节目中穿插了莲鹤方壶、妇好鸮尊、贾湖骨笛、《簪花仕女图》等国宝文物，如同唐朝少女的“博物馆奇妙夜”之旅。

《唐宫夜宴》的舞台场景充盈着古典意象元素，使观众

Night Banquet in the Tang Dynasty Palace

The dance show *Night Banquet in the Tang Dynasty Palace* is an all-female group dance played at the 2021 Spring Festival gala broadcast by the Henan Satellite Television Station. It tells the story of a group of musicians preparing for and performing at a night banquet in the Tang court. The dance is inspired by the burial figurines of musicians and dancers of the Sui Dynasty collected at the Henan Museum.

The dancers in the show, wearing costumes resembling Tang tri-colored pottery and crescent-shaped makeup, look like the figurines coming to life. Showcasing the beautiful Central Plains culture to the full, the dance is a mind-blowing visual masterpiece thanks to the use of 5G and AR technologies that put virtual scenes on the stage. Along with the agile movements of the dancers, the audience can also appreciate ancient paintings and artifacts with the help of modern technologies. The national treasures, such as the rectangular wine vessel with lotus and crane, the owl-shaped bronze wine vessel unearthed in the Tomb of Fu Hao, the Jiahu Bone Flute, and the painting of *Ladies with Head-pinned Flowers*, make the performance a real-life version of *Night at the Museum* starring the Tang ladies.

The setting for the performance is full of classic imagery that immerses the audience in a cultural atmosphere

置身在特定的中华文化框架内，在观看中成为“文化共同体”，回归共同的精神家园。节目创造出“境生象外”的美感，与文物活化重现结合，通过赏心悦目的镜头画面、张弛有致的叙事节奏和匠心独运的艺术结构来讲述主人公故事，实现审美性、艺术性、真实性的有机结合。2022年9月，《唐宫夜宴》入选“2021十大年度国家IP”。

and evokes in them a sense of cultural community shared by all Chinese. The interplay between the real and the virtual, the ingenious re-creation of the artifacts, the delightful images, and the well-paced storytelling make a perfect show of aesthetic, artistic and realistic greatness all at once. In September 2022, the dance show was selected as one of the 2021 Top Ten National IPs.

钧瓷·汝瓷

河南盛产瓷器，中国“汝、官、哥、钧、定”五大名瓷中的钧瓷和汝瓷均来自河南。

钧瓷始创于唐，盛于北宋，出产于河南省禹州市，是中国传统制瓷工艺中的珍品，素有“黄金有价钧无价”的美誉。钧瓷的神奇在于窑变艺术，钧釉在高温下熔融流动，乳浊和着色色彩发生复杂的交错变化，而使釉色变得绚丽多彩，改变了以前中国高温颜色釉只有黑釉和青釉的局面，开拓了新的艺术境界。2008年，钧瓷烧制技艺被列入国家级非物质文化遗产名录。

汝瓷是宋朝汝窑烧制的青瓷统称，因出产于河南省汝州市而得名，在陶瓷史上素有“汝窑为魁”之称。汝瓷烧制开始于唐朝中期，在北宋时达到鼎盛。汝瓷产品以天青色为基调，有天青、天蓝、月白等釉色，坯胎以香灰色和灰白色为

Jun Porcelain and Ru Porcelain

Henan Province abounds in porcelain. The Jun and the Ru, two of the five famous porcelain styles in China – Ru, Guan, Ge, Jun and Ding porcelains, both originated in Henan.

The Jun porcelain originated in the Tang Dynasty and thrived in the Northern Song Dynasty. Produced in Yuzhou, it is a shining star in China's traditional porcelain-making art and is generally considered more valuable than gold. The magic of the Jun porcelain lies in its glaze transmutation. The glaze fuses and flows at high temperatures and becomes colorful under the interplay between emulsion and coloring. This largely diversifies the high-temperature colored glaze, which used to have only two colors – black and celadon, and breaks a new horizon in this art. In 2008, the Jun porcelain-making technique was included in the list of national intangible cultural heritage.

Known as the "Champion of Porcelain," the Ru porcelain is a generalization for all celadon baked at the Ru kiln in the Northern Song Dynasty. It got its name from the place of production in Ruzhou. The Ru porcelain was first fired in the mid-Tang Dynasty and reached its peak in the Northern Song Dynasty. With celeste as the basic tone, it also comes in azure, bluish white, and other colors, while the base is in ashy gray or grayish white. The exquisite

主，以其工艺精湛、造型秀美、釉面蕴润、高雅素净的风韵而独具风采，是中国青瓷发展史上一个划时代的重要标志。2011年，汝瓷烧制技艺入选国家级非物质文化遗产名录。

craftsmanship, graceful shape, and mellow glaze make the Ru porcelain an epoch-making signature in China's celadon history. In 2011, the Ru porcelain-making technique was included in the list of national intangible cultural heritage.

四大怀药

四大怀药是河南特产，主要指古怀庆府（今河南省焦作辖区博爱、温县、沁阳、武陟、孟州等地）所产的山药、牛膝、地黄、菊花等四种中药。中国最早的药物学经典《神农本草经》把它们列为上品，之后历代医药名家进一步发现了它们的优秀本性，“四大怀药”因而流传成说，成为品牌。

怀山药能滋补益肾、健胃化痰、补中益气、祛冷风、镇心神、安魂魄、长肌髓；怀牛膝含有大量生物碱，可以补肝益肾、强壮筋骨、通经络、散恶血；怀地黄可以填骨髓、生精血、补五脏、通血脉、利耳目、黑须发；怀菊花具有散风清热、平肝明目、清热解毒的功效。

四大怀药有极高的药用和食用价值，是中国传统的常

Four Renowned Huai Medicines

These refer to the four Chinese herbal medicines growing in ancient Huaiqing (part of present-day Jiaozuo, Henan Province): Chinese yam, chaff flower root, glutinous rehmannia, and chrysanthemum. *Shen Nong Ben Cao Jing* (*Shennong's Classic of Materia Medica*), China's first medicinal classic, rated them as premium herbs, and doctors and pharmacists later found out more about their properties. These medicines consequently came to be known as an established brand.

The Huai yam can nourish the kidneys, strengthen the stomach, clear phlegm, treat asthenia and deficiency in energy, dispel the cold wind, calm the mind, and help muscles grow. The Huai chaff flower root contains a large amount of alkaloid, which is good for the liver, the kidneys, the muscles, and the bones and can unblock the meridian channels and remove blood stasis. The Huai glutinous rehmannia can make bone marrow and blood grow, nourish the five organs (heart, liver, spleen, lungs, and kidneys), invigorate blood circulation, benefit the ears and the eyes, and keep the hair black. The Huai chrysanthemum can help clear internal cold and heat, benefit the liver and the eyes, and remove pathogenic elements from the body.

With high medicinal and dietary value, these four medicines have enjoyed long-standing reputation and a

用中药材，久负盛名，畅销世界各地。其中，怀山药被誉为“怀参”“华药”，作为高级滋补品和馈赠佳品而誉满全球。

ready market around the world. Among them, the Huai yam is hailed as the "Huai ginseng" and "medicine of China" for its great nourishing effects.

信阳毛尖

中国绿茶信阳毛尖，产于河南省大别山区的信阳市浉河区（原信阳市）、平桥区（原信阳县）和罗山县。这里地势高峻、峰峦叠翠，一年四季常常云雾弥漫，年平均气温在15℃左右，年平均降水量在1200毫米上下，肥沃的土壤、深厚的腐殖质，为茶树的生长提供了充足的养分。

信阳毛尖品质高上，外形细秀匀直，色泽翠绿，内质汤色嫩绿鲜亮，香气鲜嫩高爽，叶底嫩绿明亮细嫩。其含有粗纤维、茶多酚、咖啡因等成分，对抗菌消炎、降血压、降血脂、提神醒脑、清热解毒、清心明目、增强免疫力等有辅助功效。

信阳茶叶种植历史悠久，从唐朝开始，茶叶生产便进入兴盛时期，所产茶叶品质上乘，列为贡品。“茶圣”陆羽在《茶经》中把信阳毛尖列为唐朝名茶。宋朝大文学家苏东坡曾说，“淮南茶，信阳第一”。信阳毛尖于1915年荣获巴

Xinyang Maojian Tea

Maojian is a kind of green tea that grows on the steep Dabie Mountains in Xinyang, Henan Province. Shrouded by lush trees and perennial clouds and fogs, the mountains have an average annual temperature of 15 degrees Celsius and an average annual rainfall of 1,200 millimeters, which, coupled with the fertile soil and deep humus, provide the tea trees with adequate nourishment.

Xinyang Maojian tea boasts high quality, slender bright green leaves, transparent green soup, and refreshing fragrance. Containing coarse fiber, tea polyphenols, and caffeine, it can help counter bacteria and inflammation, reduce blood pressure and blood fat, refresh the mind, clear internal heat and pathogenic factors, reduce eye fatigue, and boost immunity.

Xinyang has a long history of tea planting. Local tea production bloomed in the Tang Dynasty, and the tea leaves were selected as a tribute to the imperial court for their superior quality. Lu Yu (733-c. 804), the Sage of Tea, put Xinyang Maojian on the list of best teas of the Tang Dynasty in his *Cha Jing* (*Classic of Tea*). Su Dongpo (1037-1101), a great literary master of the Song Dynasty, praised the Xinyang tea "the best in the south of the Huaihe River."

Xinyang Maojian won a gold medal at the 1915 Panama Pacific International Exposition and was rated one

拿马万国博览会金奖，1958年被评为中国十大名茶之一。2014年，信阳毛尖茶制作技艺入选国家级非物质文化遗产名录。

of the 10 best teas in China in 1958. In 2014, the Xinyang Maojian tea processing technique was put on the list of national intangible cultural heritage.

河南烩面

河南烩面是河南省的一道特色面食，有着悠久的历史，是一种荤、素、汤、菜、饭兼而有之的传统风味小吃，与北京炸酱面、山西刀削面、湖北热干面、四川担担面、兰州牛肉面并称中国著名面食，享有盛誉。

河南烩面以优质高筋面粉为原料，辅以高汤及海带丝、千张丝、粉条、鹌鹑蛋等多种配菜，上桌时再外带香菜、辣椒油、糖蒜等小碟。按照配料的不同，可分为：羊肉烩面、牛肉烩面、三鲜烩面、五鲜烩面等。烩面之香在于汤，汤是由羊肉和羊腿骨熬成的，加入党参、当归、黄芪、白芷、枸杞等中药，既去了羊肉的膻气，又消减了羊肉的火气，是上等滋补佳品。

河南烩面面香肉烂，味道浓郁，经济实惠，已经成为中原地区最典型的风味小吃之一。对于河南人来说，烩面不仅

Henan Stewed Noodles

This is a local food with noodles, meat, vegetables, and soup all in one. With a long history, it is one of the most famous noodles in China along with Beijing's noodles with fried soy sauce and minced meat, Shanxi's sliced noodles, Hubei's hot dry noodles with sesame sauce, Sichuan's noodles with chili sauce, and Lanzhou's hand-pulled beef noodles.

Henan stewed noodles are made of high-protein flour, cooked with various trimmings such as well-boiled soup, shredded kelp, slices of dried bean curd, starch noodles, and quail eggs, and served with side dishes like coriander, chili oil, and sweetened garlic. Given the different trimmings, there are mutton noodles, beef noodles, and assorted noodles. Their fragrance comes from the soup, which is cooked with mutton and lamb leg bones, and the addition of Chinese medicinal herbs such as *dangshen* (codonopsis root), *danggui* (Chinese angelica), *huangqi* (milkvetch root), *baizhi* (dehurian angelica root), and *gouqi* (wolfberry) helps remove the raw smell of mutton and neutralizes its heat, resulting in a highly tonic dish.

Henan stewed noodles are a typical dish in the Central Plains popular for being tasty and fair priced. For the locals, it is more than just a dish: It represents their love for their hometown. The noodles were served at the banquet for the

是一种美食，还是一种情感。2015年，上海合作组织成员国总理第十四次会议在河南省郑州市举行，宴席中的一道特色菜品就是河南烩面。

14th meeting of the Council of Heads of Government (Prime Ministers) of the Shanghai Cooperation Organization held in Zhengzhou in 2015.

道口烧鸡

道口烧鸡是河南省安阳市的一道传统名菜，始创于清顺治十八年（公元1661年），成型于清乾隆时期，经过几百年的传承与发展，道口烧鸡已经成为与北京烤鸭、金华火腿齐名的中国名菜。

据传，道口烧鸡由滑县道口镇“义兴张”烧鸡店所制，开始制作不得法，生意并不兴隆，后从清宫御膳房的御厨处求得制作烧鸡秘方，做出的烧鸡十分香美。道口烧鸡的制作技艺由此历代相传，并逐渐形成其独特风格。

道口烧鸡之所以享誉海内外，关键在于它精细的制作工艺。其使用多种中药辅之陈年老汤，成品烧鸡色泽鲜艳，极具食疗和保健功能。老汤就是煮鸡的陈汤，每煮一锅鸡，必须加上头锅的老汤，如此沿袭，越老越好。单单煮鸡一道程序便需要花上3至5个小时，再加上火候的调整，制作技术要求很高。

Daokou Red-Cooked Chicken

The Daokou red-cooked chicken is a traditional dish of Anyang, Henan Province. Created in 1661 during the Qing Dynasty, the dish, with improvements over hundreds of years, now enjoys equal fame in China as Beijing roast duck and Jinhua ham.

It is said that the chicken was first cooked by the Yixingzhang restaurant in Daokou Town, Huaxian County. At first, the chicken did not sell very well. Later the owner got a recipe from a royal cook to make mouth-watering chicken, which was passed down from generation to generation with a distinctive local flavor added.

The Daokou red-cooked chicken's fame should be attributed to its meticulous cooking process. The use of multiple Chinese medicinal herbs and the long-cooked soup give the chicken a bright color and good therapeutic and tonic effects. It takes three to five hours to prepare the soup, not to mention the well-timed adjustment of the fire, which requires rich experience and a high level of expertise.

红旗渠

红旗渠位于河南省安阳市林州市，是20世纪60年代林县（今林州市）人民为了解决千百年来干旱缺水的难题，在太行山悬崖峭壁上修建的引漳入林的水利工程。红旗渠全长1500千米，参与修建人数近10万，耗时近10年（1960—1969）。该工程共削平了1250座山头，架设151座渡槽，开凿211个隧洞，修建各种建筑物12408座，挖砌土石达2225万立方米。如把这些土石垒筑成高2米、宽3米的墙，可纵贯祖国南北，把广州与哈尔滨连接起来。

红旗渠的建成彻底改善了林县人民靠天等雨的恶劣生存环境，结束了林县十年九旱、水贵如油的苦难历史，红旗渠被当地人民称为“生命渠”“幸福渠”，也被誉为“人工天河”“新中国奇迹”“世界水利第八大奇迹”。在当时三年自然灾害和国家经济困难的大背景下，林县人民以愚公移山精神，自带工具，自备口粮，风餐露宿，靠着“一锤、一钎、一双手”，创造出太行山上的人间奇迹，孕育了“自力更生，艰苦创业，团结协作，无私奉献”的红旗渠精神。

Hongqi Canal

The Hongqi Canal is a water conservancy project in Linzhou, Anyang of Henan Province. From 1960 to 1969, to solve the water shortage that had troubled the locality for hundreds of years, the people of Linxian County (present-day Linzhou) spent nearly 10 years digging a 1,500-kilometer-long canal on the cliffs of the Taihang Mountains. About 100,000 people joined the project: They flattened 1,250 hills, erected 151 aqueducts, dug through 211 tunnels, built 12,408 structures of various kinds, and used 22.25 million cubic meters of earth and stone.

The Hongqi Canal improved the Linxian people's living environment and ended their long history of dire water scarcity due to frequent drought. The canal was therefore called by the locals a "canal of life" and "canal of happiness" and also reputed as a "man-made heavenly river," a "miracle of China," and the "eighth wonder in the world history of water conservancy projects." It was built at a time when China suffered from natural disasters over three consecutive years and great economic difficulties, but the Linxian people, in the spirit of the mountain-moving Yu Gong, worked a wonder on the Taihang Mountains against unimaginable obstacles just with hammers, drill rods, and their hands. The self-reliance, endurance, unity, cooperation, and selfless dedication they displayed during this large-scale

改革开放以来，林州人民不断赋予红旗渠精神新的内涵，将中华民族艰苦奋斗的传统美德与时代精神结合起来，谱写了气壮山河的“战太行、出太行、富太行”创业三部曲，实现了林州由山区贫困县向现代化新兴城市、生态旅游城市的跨越。

project have given birth to the spirit of the Hongqi Canal.

Since the reform and opening up began in the late 1970s, the local people have injected new elements into this spirit, combining the Chinese nation's traditional virtue of hard work with the realities of the new era. Working in this spirit, they have turned Linzhou from an impoverished mountainous county into a modern place supported by eco-tourism.

焦裕禄

焦裕禄，河南省兰考县原县委书记，中国县委书记的榜样。焦裕禄于1946年加入中国共产党，于1962年被调到兰考县担任县委书记。

1962年12月至1964年间，兰考县遭受严重的内涝、风沙、盐碱“三害”。焦裕禄坚持实事求是、群众路线的工作方法，同全县干部和群众一起治理“三害”，立誓“拼上老命大干一场，决心改变兰考面貌”。由于繁重的工作和长期不规律的饮食，焦裕禄身患肝癌，但他用硬物顶着肝部缓解疼痛，坚持工作。他与时间赛跑，与自然灾害抗争，奋战了475天，用生命换取兰考人民的幸福。1964年5月，焦裕禄病逝于郑州，终年42岁。

在焦裕禄精神的感召下，兰考县的干部群众齐心协力，有效治理了“三害”。1965年，历史上一直缺粮的兰考实现了粮食自给自足。2017年，兰考县退出贫困县序列，成为河南首个“摘帽”的贫困县，也是全国第一批实现脱贫的国家级贫困县。多年来，每年有成千上万的人从世界各地前来

Jiao Yulu

Jiao Yulu (1922-1964) was secretary of the Party Committee of Lankao County, Henan Province and a role model for all county Party committee secretaries in China. He joined the Communist Party of China (CPC) in 1946 and came to work in Lankao in 1962.

Lankao County suffered from three serious harms – waterlogging, sandstorms, and land salinization. Jiao Yulu, following the principles of seeking truth from facts and relying on the people, worked shoulder to shoulder with the officials and local people in an all-out effort to improve Lankao's outlook. Because of onerous work and irregular meals over a long time, he was diagnosed with liver cancer, but he kept on working notwithstanding, racing against time to combat natural disasters. He worked tirelessly for 475 days and devoted his life to the well-being of Lankao's people. In May 1964, he died of cancer in Zhengzhou at the age of 42.

Inspired by Jiao Yulu, the officials and the people of Lankao County continued their effort and succeeded in harnessing the "three harms." In 1965, the county achieved self-sufficiency in grain production. In 2017, it was removed from the list of impoverished counties, the first in the province and one of the first in the country. Every year, tens of thousands of people travel to Lankao to commemorate

缅怀焦裕禄，参观学习兰考县的巨大发展变化。

2009年到2014年，习近平三次到兰考指导工作，把焦裕禄精神概括为“亲民爱民、艰苦奋斗、科学求实、迎难而上、无私奉献”，并号召学习焦裕禄同志的“三股劲”：对群众的那股亲劲、抓工作的那股韧劲、干事业的那股拼劲。

Jiao Yulu and learn from Lankao's experience of making tremendous changes.

From 2009 to 2014, Xi Jinping inspected Lankao three times. He summed up Jiao Yulu's spirit as "loving the people, working hard against difficulties, respecting science and seeking truth, and making selfless contributions" and called on the officials and Party members to learn three things from him – how he kept in close touch with the people, how tenacious he was at work, and how determined he was in serving the people.

展望河南篇

III

黄河流域生态保护和高质量发展

保护黄河是事关中华民族伟大复兴和永续发展的千秋大计。治理黄河，重在保护，要在治理。中共十八大以来，黄河流域生态保护、经济发展、产业融合、城市群和中心城市建设、乡村振兴等方面取得诸多成绩，初步实现了量和质的融合发展。

2019年9月，习近平在河南省郑州市主持召开黄河流域生态保护和高质量发展座谈会时强调，黄河流域是中国重要的生态屏障和重要的经济地带，在国家经济社会发展和生态安全方面具有十分重要的地位。2021年10月，中共中央、国务院印发《黄河流域生态保护和高质量发展规划纲要》，对流域生态保护和高质量发展过程的重点方向、关键要素、发展模式、政策措施、支撑体系等进行了纲领性规划。

在黄河流域生态保护和高质量发展这一重大国家战略指引下，沿黄各省区正进一步高效推动产业绿色发展，强化创新资源与生产要素的高效融合，以真正实现黄河流域高质量

Ecological Protection and High-Quality Development of the Yellow River Basin

Protecting the Yellow River concerns the rejuvenation and sustainable development of the Chinese nation. In harnessing the Yellow River, protection and governance assume equal importance. Since the 18th National Congress of the CPC in 2012, progress both in quantity and quality has been achieved in the Yellow River basin in terms of eco-protection, economic development, industrial integration, construction of city clusters and central cities, and rural revitalization.

In September 2019, Xi Jinping presided over a meeting in Zhengzhou on the eco-protection and high-quality development of the Yellow River basin. He emphasized the basin's pivotal role as a vital ecological screen and economic belt in China's socioeconomic development and ecological security. In October 2021, the CPC Central Committee and the State Council issued the Outline of the Ecological Protection and High-quality Development Plan of the Yellow River Basin, which laid out the priorities, key factors, development model, policies and measures, and supporting systems for the endeavors.

To implement this national plan, the nine provinces and autonomous regions along the Yellow River are accelerating green industrial development and further aligning innovative resources with production factors for

发展。

河南省在黄河流域以及新发展格局中的地位举足轻重。河南省承载了全国1亿多人口、全国1/4的小麦产量和全国1/10的粮食产量，承担着保障国家粮食安全的重大任务。河南省沿黄区域是地形地貌特征最为特殊的地区，在黄河全流域生态文明建设中肩负了特殊使命和艰巨任务。黄河流域生态保护和高质量发展上升为重大国家战略以来，河南省提出打造黄河生态保护示范区、黄河高质量发展引领区、黄河文化传承创新区，强化创新动力，加快建设绿色制造体系和服务体系，逐步构建以郑州都市圈建设为核心引擎的都市圈一体化发展体制机制。

high-quality development.

Henan holds an important position in the Yellow River basin and China's new development dynamic. With a population of more than 100 million and producing one quarter of wheat and one tenth of grain for the country, the province plays an irreplaceable part in ensuring national food security. The unique landforms along the Yellow River set the riverside regions an arduous task in promoting ecological conservation in the river basin. Since the basin's eco-protection and high-quality development was made a major national strategy, Henan has set the goals to develop an eco-protection demonstration zone, a high-quality development pioneer zone, and a zone for preservation and innovative development of the Yellow River culture. It will rely more on innovation as a driving force and move faster to establish green manufacturing and service systems in pursuit of integrated development of city clusters powered by the construction of the Zhengzhou metropolitan area.

“打好四张牌”

2014年5月，习近平在河南省考察时提出希望河南省围绕加快转变经济发展方式和提高经济整体素质及竞争力，着力打好以发展优势产业为主导推进产业结构优化升级，以构建自主创新体系为主导推进创新驱动发展，以强化基础能力建设为主导推进培育发展新优势，以人为核心推进新型城镇化的“四张牌”，着力解决好教育、就业、社会保障、医疗卫生等人民群众的切身利益问题，在拓展更大更广发展空间的同时，努力让人民过上更好的生活。“打好四张牌”把准了河南省发展脉搏，切中河南省发展的突出矛盾和重大关键问题，符合河南省发展实际，具有很强的思想性、战略性、针对性和指导性。

河南省把“打好四张牌”作为落实新发展理念、深化供给侧结构性改革、推进高质量发展的关键举措，奋力推动发展优势转化为发展胜势、汇聚成发展强势，推动社会经济

Four Strong Cards for Henan's Development

During his inspection of Henan in May 2014, Xi Jinping urged the province to play its "four cards" well with a view to accelerating the transformation of the economic growth model and improving the overall quality and competitiveness of the economy. The "four cards" refer to optimizing and upgrading the industrial structure by developing advantageous industries, promoting innovation-driven development by building an independent innovation system, fostering new development strengths by enhancing basic capabilities, and advancing people-centered new urbanization. In this process, Henan needs to address issues of immediate concern to the people, such as education, employment, social security, and medical and health care, so that the people will enjoy a better life as the province expands its space for development.

Xi's remarks on the "four cards" provide effective strategic guidance to Henan as they target the prominent problems and key issues in its development and match its reality. To play these four cards well will support the province in implementing the new development philosophy, deepening the supply-side structural reform, and promoting high-quality development. The province has endeavored to turn its strengths into a sustained driving force for healthy and rapid socioeconomic development.

健康快速发展。目前，河南省以制造业高质量发展为主攻方向，统筹推进传统产业绿色转型、主导产业扩容提质和新兴产业培育壮大，装备制造、食品制造正在跃向万亿级产业，人工智能、数字经济带来新的活力，产业结构实现由“二三一”到“三二一”的历史性转变；把科技创新作为第一动力，郑洛新国家自主创新示范区引领作用不断增强，国家生物育种产业创新中心、国家农机装备创新中心获批建设，国家超级计算郑州中心建成投用，发展动能显著增强；着力构建连通境内外、辐射东中西的物流通道枢纽、现代立体综合交通枢纽和引领未来的新型基础设施体系，河南物流业已迈入全国第一方阵；加快构建以人为核心、以中原城市群为主体、大中小城市和小城镇协调发展的现代城镇体系。

At present, Henan is focusing on high-quality manufacturing development, propelling the green transformation of traditional industries, expanding and upgrading leading industries, and cultivating and strengthening emerging ones. Its equipment manufacturing and food-making industries are producing an output value of one trillion yuan, AI and digital economy are generating new vitality, and industrial structure has made a historic change from being dominated by secondary industry to by tertiary industry. While taking technological innovation as the primary driving force, the province is seeing the Zhengzhou-Luoyang-Xinxiang National Innovation Demonstration Zone playing a leading role, the National Bio-breeding Innovation Center and the National Agricultural Machinery and Equipment Innovation Center under construction, and the National Supercomputing Center in Zhengzhou coming into operation upon completion. This has added a stronger impetus to local development. Henan is working to build a logistics hub connecting Chinese and foreign markets and linking China's eastern, central and western regions. It is also building a modern comprehensive and multi-dimensional transportation hub and future-oriented, new-type infrastructure. This will further benefit its logistics industry that is already one of the best in China. The province is also quickening its pace to build a people-centered modern urban system focusing on the Central Plains cities and featuring coordinated development of large, medium-sized and small cities as well as small towns.

河南省还聚焦装备制造、绿色食品、新型材料、电子信息、节能环保、现代轻纺、绿色建材、汽车制造、生物医药、现代化工等重点产业，预期到2025年，全省产业基础能力和产业链现代化水平达到国内一流，形成数个万亿级产业集群、一批千亿级新兴产业集群和百亿级企业。

Henan is taking steps in an array of key industries, including equipment manufacturing, green food, new materials, electronic information, energy conservation and environmental protection, modern textiles, green building materials, auto-making, biomedicine, and modern chemical industry. It is expected that by 2025, the province's basic industrial capacity and industrial chain modernization will lead the country, with several industrial clusters with an annual output value exceeding one trillion yuan, a number of emerging industrial clusters with an annual output value exceeding 100 billion yuan, and a group of enterprises with an annual output value exceeding 10 billion yuan.

“两个确保”

2021年10月，中共河南省第十一次党代会立足河南发展新的历史起点，以前瞻30年的眼光，明确提出锚定“两个确保”（确保高质量建设现代化河南，确保高水平实现现代化河南）的奋斗目标。

按照“两个确保”的要求，到2035年河南省要基本建成经济强省、文化强省、生态强省、开放强省和国家创新高地、幸福美好家园，到21世纪中叶建成富强、民主、文明、和谐、美丽的社会主义现代化强省。其指标体系主要包括经济发展、创新驱动、民生福祉和绿色生态四个方面。到2035年，人均GDP要达到2万美元，城镇化率达到72%，劳动年龄人口平均受教育年限达到12年，人均预期寿命达到80岁，非化石能源消费占比达到30%以上，全员劳动生产率、研发经费投入、人均可支配收入达到全国平均水平。在此基础上，一流创新生态基本形成，主导产业生态体系基本形成，新型基础设施体系基本形成，城乡融合发展格局基

Two Goals for Mid-21st Century Henan

The long-range goals, set at the provincial congress of CPC delegates in October 2021, are to build a modern Henan with high quality and high standards by the mid-21st century.

To be specific, by 2035 Henan will become a province strong in economy, culture, ecology, and opening up, a national highland of innovation, and a happy home for the people, and by the middle of this century become a great modern socialist province that is prosperous, strong, democratic, culturally advanced, harmonious, and beautiful. There are four indicators to measure whether the goals are achieved – economic development, innovation drive, people's well-being, and green ecology.

By 2035, Henan's per capita GDP will reach 20,000 US dollars, urbanization rate will reach 72 percent, its working-age population will receive 12 years of education on average, the average life expectancy will reach 80 years, non-fossil energy will make up over 30 percent of energy consumption, and the overall labor productivity, R&D investment, and per capita disposable income will reach the national average level. On that basis, a first-class innovation environment, a system of leading industries, a new-type infrastructure system, a pattern of integrated urban-rural development, and supporting institutions and mechanisms

本形成，支持高质量发展的体制机制基本形成；对外开放能级显著提高，生态环境质量显著提高，文化发展质量显著提高，人民生活品质显著提高，管党治党水平显著提高。

“两个确保”描绘了中国式现代化在河南实践的新图景，开启了具有时代特征、凸显河南特点的现代化建设新征程。

for high-quality development will all basically take form. Henan's opening up to the outside world will be on a much higher level, and the quality of its ecological environment, cultural development, people's lives, and Party governance will also all be significantly improved.

These two goals map out the new vista of Henan along with the Chinese modernization and kick off the province's new journey of modernization bearing the imprints of the times and local features.

“十大战略”

2021年10月，中共河南省第十一次党代会明确提出，锚定“两个确保”，必须全面实施“十大战略”，通过实施一大批变革性、牵引性、标志性举措来育先机、开新局。“十大战略”是河南省实现“两个确保”目标的战略方向、战略重点和战略路径。

实施创新驱动、科教兴省、人才强省战略。把创新摆在发展的逻辑起点、现代化建设的核心位置，做强创新平台，壮大创新主体，集聚创新人才，完善创新制度，优化创新生态，建设国家创新高地。

实施优势再造战略。推动交通区位优势向枢纽经济优势、产业基础优势向现代产业体系优势、内需规模优势向产业链供应链协同优势转变，形成高质量发展新动能。

实施数字化转型战略。突出数字化引领、撬动、赋能作用，加快构建系统完备、高效实用、智能绿色、安全可靠的

Ten Strategies

To achieve the two mid-21st century goals, Henan will implement 10 strategies and foster opportunities to break a new horizon by carrying out a raft of pioneering and symbolic reform measures. The 10 strategies are the priorities leading to Henan's modernization.

Strategy for driving development with innovation and strengthening the province with science, education, and workforce development. Prioritizing innovation in provincial development and modernization, Henan will strengthen the innovation platforms, enlarge the group of innovators, pool innovative talent, and improve relevant systems and conditions in an endeavor to build a national highland of innovation.

Strategy for strength recreation. Making the best of its geographical location in central China, its strong industrial foundation, and large demand from a large population, Henan is working to develop an economic hub, a modern industrial system, and coordinated industrial and supply chains, so as to forge new drives for high-quality development.

Digital transformation strategy. Leveraging the leading and empowering role of digital technologies, Henan is moving faster to develop a new-type infrastructure system that is sound, efficient, practical, intelligent, green, and safe,

新型基础设施体系，壮大数字核心产业，推进传统产业数字化改造，全面提升数治能力。

实施换道领跑战略。在传统产业上高位嫁接，在新兴产业上抢滩占先，在未来产业上前瞻布局，全面提升产业竞争力。

实施文旅文创融合战略。发展富有特色的全链条文旅业态，壮大以创意为内核的文化产业，打造中华文化传承创新中心、世界文化旅游胜地。

实施以人为核心的新型城镇化战略。坚持从社会全面进步和人的全面发展出发，科学编制国土空间规划，推动中原城市群一体化高质量发展，加快构建主副引领、四区协同、多点支撑的发展格局，使城市更健康、更安全、更宜居，打造高品质生活空间。

实施乡村振兴战略。毫不放松抓好粮食生产，以产业链、价值链、供应链“三链同构”提升农业效益和竞争力、促进农民增收，以实施乡村建设行动为抓手建设美丽乡村，加快建设现代农业强省。

stimulate the core digital economy industries, and push forward digitalization of traditional industries to enhance its capability of digital governance across the board.

Strategy for leading in new tracks. Henan will upgrade its traditional industries by applying advanced technologies, seize the critical opportunity to gain an edge in emerging industries, and make forward-looking plans for industries of the future to enhance its overall industrial competitiveness.

Strategy for integrating recreational tourism with cultural creativity. Henan will develop distinctive recreational tourism, scale up the cultural industry with creativity at the core, and create a center for the preservation and innovation of the Chinese culture and an international destination of cultural tourism.

Strategy for people-centered new urbanization. Aiming at all-round social progress and human development, Henan has developed a science-based territorial space plan which promotes high-quality integrated development of city clusters and the formation of a well-conceived development pattern, in order to build healthy, safe and livable cities where people can enjoy better lives.

Rural revitalization strategy. Henan will continue to promote its grain production and increase its agricultural benefits and competitiveness and farmers' income by integrating the industrial, value and supply chains. It has launched a campaign to build a beautiful countryside and is taking bigger steps to build a strong modern agriculture.

实施绿色低碳转型战略。以推进碳达峰碳中和为牵引，坚持绿色生产、绿色技术、绿色生活、绿色制度一体推进，全面提升能源安全绿色保障水平，建立健全绿色低碳循环发展的经济体系。

实施制度型开放战略。对标对接国际贸易和投资通行规则，构建稳定透明可预期的开放政策制度体系，提高开放型经济发展水平。

实施全面深化改革战略。发挥改革服务构建新发展格局的关键作用，在全面上做文章、深化上下功夫，实现改革举措有机衔接、有效贯通、有序联动。

Strategy for green and low-carbon transformation. Guided by China's goal of carbon peaking and carbon neutrality, Henan will promote green production, green technologies, green life, and green systems in parallel, provide greater green energy security, and establish a sound green, low-carbon circular economy.

Strategy for institutional opening up. Henan will align its own rules with international trade and investment rules and put in place a stable, transparent, and predictable system of policies and institutions to develop a higher-standard open economy.

Strategy for comprehensive reform. Henan will give full play to reform as the key element in forming a new development dynamic and deepen the reform comprehensively to make sure that relevant measures are well aligned and effectively coordinated.

郑洛新国家自主创新示范区

2016年3月，国务院常务会议确定新设河南郑洛新、山东半岛、辽宁沈大3个国家自主创新示范区。同年5月，中共河南省委、河南省人民政府印发《郑洛新国家自主创新示范区建设实施方案》，从总体要求、战略定位、空间布局和功能布局、发展目标、重点任务、保障措施等方面对郑洛新国家自主创新示范区建设进行了全面安排部署。

郑洛新国家自主创新示范区是中原地区的高科技产业中心和河南省体制机制创新的重要示范基地，依托郑州、洛阳、新乡3个城市高新技术产业开发区，举全省之力将其建设成为具有较强辐射能力和核心竞争力的创新高地。截至2020年年底，郑洛新三市高新技术企业总数达3883家、国家科技型中小企业入库数量达7823家，分别占全省的61.3%和66.2%；万人发明专利拥有量达12.29件，是全省平均水平的3.2倍；技术合同成交额达306.8亿元，占全省的79.8%以上；高新技术产业增加值占规上工业增加值比重达57.4%，高于全省平均水平14个百分点；培育、集聚了

Zhengzhou-Luoyang-Xinxiang National Innovation Demonstration Zone

The Zhengzhou-Luoyang-Xinxiang National Innovation Demonstration Zone was approved by the State Council in March 2016. This was followed by a detailed development plan jointly released in May by the CPC Henan Provincial Committee and the People's Government of Henan Province. The document made overall arrangements for the endeavor, including main requirements, strategic position, spatial and functional layout, objectives, key tasks, and supporting measures.

The Zhengzhou-Luoyang-Xinxiang zone is a high-tech industrial center in the Central Plains and an important base for Henan's institutional innovation. Based on the new- and high-tech industrial development zones in the three cities, this zone is expected to become a highland of innovation with a strong driving power and core competitiveness.

By the end of 2020, the three cities had 3,883 high-tech enterprises and 7,823 national sci-tech SMEs, both accounting for about two-thirds of the province's total number. The invention patents they hold per 10,000 people reached 12.29, 3.2 times the provincial average; technology contract turnover reached 30.68 billion yuan, accounting for 79.8 percent of the provincial total; and the added value from high-tech sectors accounted for 57.4 percent of that of all large industrial enterprises, 14 percentage points higher

全省60%的国家级创新平台、61%的高新技术企业、50%的创新型龙头企业、2/3的科技型中小企业和80%以上的国家重点实验室，成为引领全省创新发展的核心增长极。

than the provincial average. The three cities also gathered 60 percent of Henan's national innovation platforms, 61 percent of its high-tech enterprises, 50 percent of its leading innovation companies, two-thirds of its sci-tech SMEs, and over 80 percent of its national key labs. They are the core growth poles in the province's innovation-driven development.

南水北调中线工程

南水北调工程是世界上规模最大的调水工程，东、中、西线干线规划总长度达4350千米，构成以“四横三纵”为主体的总体布局，以实现中国水资源南北调配、东西互济的合理配置格局。其中，中线工程从汉江中上游横跨湖北和河南两省的丹江口水库取汉江水，输水干渠地跨河南、河北、北京、天津4个省、直辖市，一期工程于2003年年底开工，2014年12月正式通水。

中线工程全长1432千米，沟通长江、淮河、黄河、海河四大流域，穿过黄河干流及其他集流面积10平方千米以上河流219条，跨越铁路44处，需建跨总干渠的公路桥571座。其中，穿黄隧洞是南水北调工程中规模最大、单项工期最长、技术含量最高、施工难度最复杂的交叉建筑物。在中

Middle Route of the South-to-North Water Diversion Project

The South-to-North Water Diversion Project is the largest of its kind in the world with its eastern, middle and western routes measuring 4,350 kilometers in total and a massive network of these three vertical routes connecting four major rivers. The project is designed to divert the water resources between the south and the north, the east and the west for a relatively reasonable redistribution.

The middle route draws water from the Danjiangkou Reservoir, which is located in the middle and upper reaches of the Hanjiang River, a tributary of the Yangtze. The canal water runs through two provinces (Henan and Hebei) and two municipalities (Beijing and Tianjin). Phase I of the middle route started construction at the end of 2003, and water diversion officially began in December 2014.

The 1,432-kilometer middle route connects four river basins: Yangtze, Huaihe, Yellow, and Haihe, crosses 219 rivers that each have a drainage area of 10 square kilometers, including the trunk stream of the Yellow River, and runs beneath railways at 44 spots. A total of 571 road bridges have to be built over the main diversion channel. Of all the structures, the tunnel beneath the Yellow River is the largest, most technically demanding, and most complicated and difficult with the longest construction period for a single structure. Of all the provinces and municipalities

线工程涉及的省（市）中，河南省境内干线长度731千米，线路最长，建设任务最重，移民搬迁人数最多。

南水北调中线工程可极大地缓解中国中、北部地区的水资源短缺问题，改善受水区域的生态环境和投资环境，推动区域经济社会发展。截至2021年，南水北调中线一期工程向豫冀津京累计调水超过441亿立方米，有效缓解了地下水超采的局面，使经济发展格局得到优化，并取得十分显著的生态环境效益。

2021年9月，在“生物多样性100+案例”全球征集与评选活动中，“河南丹江南水北调中线水源地保护与修复”案例，从全球26个国家的258个申报案例中脱颖而出，成功入选“生物多样性100+全球典型案例”名单。

along the middle route, Henan possesses the longest trunk line (731 kilometers), which implies the most onerous work and the largest number of relocated people.

The middle route can largely mitigate the water scarcity in central and northern China, improve the ecological and investment environment in the water-receiving areas, and promote their socioeconomic development. By 2021, Phase I had cumulatively provided 44 billion cubic meters of water to Henan, Hebei, Tianjin, and Beijing, effectively easing their over-exploitation of underground water, bettering their economic landscape, and creating remarkable ecological and environmental benefits.

During the "100+ Biodiversity Positive Practices and Actions Around the World" campaign held in 2021, the "protection and restoration of water sources in the middle South-North water diversion route, Danjiang, Henan" was selected to be one of the global model cases, out of 258 candidates from 26 countries.

乡村振兴

实施乡村振兴战略，是新时代做好“三农”工作的重大战略部署。习近平曾对实施乡村振兴战略进行系统阐述，并多次强调乡村振兴是包括产业振兴、人才振兴、文化振兴、生态振兴、组织振兴的全面振兴，明确提出农业农村现代化是实施乡村振兴战略的总目标，坚持农业农村优先发展是总方针，产业兴旺、生态宜居、乡风文明、治理有效、生活富裕是总要求，建立健全城乡融合发展体制机制和政策体系是制度保障。

作为中国重要的农业大省、人口大省，河南坚持把“三农”工作摆在重中之重的位置，大力实施乡村振兴战略。截至2022年年底，河南农业生产稳产增效，粮食产量连续6年保持在1300亿斤以上，农产品加工业成为万亿级产业，为保障国家粮食安全持续贡献河南力量；乡村建设扎实推进，全省所有行政村通硬化路、通客车，农村集中供水率达93%，农村生活垃圾收运处置体系覆盖所有行政村，农村

Rural Revitalization

Implementing the rural revitalization strategy is a major move to improve the work relating to agriculture, rural areas, and farmers in the current era. Xi Jinping has systematically expounded on how to implement the strategy. He emphasizes that the strategy targets comprehensive progress in businesses, the workforce, culture, ecological conservation, and the organizational structure. The goal is agricultural and rural modernization, so priority will be given to agriculture and rural areas to create a countryside featuring thriving businesses, pleasant living environments, social etiquette and civility, effective governance, and affluent life. Sound institutions, mechanisms, and policies for integrated urban-rural development will provide institutional guarantee for such an effort.

A province with strong agriculture and a large population, Henan has made strenuous efforts to implement the rural revitalization strategy. Its grain output exceeded 65 billion kilograms in 2022, the sixth year in a row, and the agro-processing industry generated an output value of one trillion yuan, making sustained contributions to China's food security. The province is also making steady progress with its rural development. All administrative villages have paved roads and bus connections and are covered by the domestic waste collection and treatment system, and

人居环境整体提升，居民对村庄环境的满意度保持在90%以上；农民收入较快增长，2022年河南省农村居民人均可支配收入比上年增长6.6%，城乡居民收入比值继续缩小。

作为中国脱贫攻坚任务较重的省份，河南高质量打赢脱贫攻坚战，取得了现行标准下贫困人口全部脱贫、贫困村全部退出、贫困县全部摘帽的历史性成就。脱贫攻坚取得胜利后，中国“三农”工作重心实现历史性转移，由脱贫攻坚转向全面推进乡村振兴。为此，河南将努力扛稳粮食安全重任，在农业高质量发展上务求新提升；深化农村改革，在推进城乡融合发展上迈出新步伐；在基层治理上实现新提升，推动农业高质高效、乡村宜居宜业、农民富裕富足。

93 percent of them have a centralized water supply. The living environment has improved to the satisfaction of most residents. Farmers' income has seen a rapid increase. In 2022, the per capita disposable income of rural residents grew 6.6 percent from the previous year, further narrowing the urban-rural income gap.

Henan has fulfilled the arduous task of poverty alleviation along with the rest of the country, with rural people living below the current poverty line and poor villages and counties all eliminating absolute poverty. Following this historic accomplishment, the country has turned to promote rural revitalization across the board. In response to this shift, Henan will meet its responsibility for ensuring food security and strive for new progress in high-quality development of agriculture. It will deepen rural reform and advance urban-rural integrated development. It will further improve community-level governance and build a countryside with quality, efficient agriculture, a livable and work-friendly environment, and well-off farmers.

“中原农谷”

种子是农业的“芯片”。自古以来，种子便一直处于种植产业链的最前端，农作物的产量和质量都和种子直接相关。河南省地处中原，农耕文明悠久，粮食作物丰富，是中国重要的粮食主产区，素有“国人粮仓”美誉。中共十八大以来，河南把粮食生产摆在各项工作重中之重的位置，全面落实藏粮于地、藏粮于技战略，聚焦种子和耕地两个要害，农业生产条件和技术水平不断提高。

2022年4月，河南省人民政府印发《“中原农谷”建设方案》（以下简称《方案》），明确了“中原农谷”建设的目标要求、区域布局、重点任务和工作机制。2023年6月，河南省人民政府印发《中原农谷发展规划（2022—2035年）》（以下简称《规划》），进一步明确了“中原农谷”发展战略、政策措施、重大工程项目等。

“中原农谷”总规划面积为1611.83平方千米，总人口超过144万人。在功能定位方面，“中原农谷”聚焦建设国家级、国际化农业创新高地，大力发展生物育种、现代种养、农副产品加工、生物技术产品、农机装备制造、现代农业服

Central Plains Agricultural Valley

Seeds are the "chip" of agriculture. Since ancient times, seeds have been key in the planting industry chain, bearing directly on the output and quality of crops. Henan, with an old agro-civilization and abundant food crops, is an important breadbasket of China. It has given top priority to grain production, fully implemented the strategy on sustainable use of the arable land and application of technologies to ensure national food security, ameliorated the two key factors of seeds and soil, and continuously improved the conditions and technologies for agricultural production.

In April 2022, the provincial government unveiled a plan for developing a "Central Plains Agricultural Valley," which specified the major goals, geographical location, key tasks, and working mechanisms. In June 2023, it revealed the Development Plan for the Central Plains Agricultural Valley (2022-2035), which clarified the development strategy, policies and measures, and major projects.

The Central Plains Agricultural Valley has a planned area of 1,611 square kilometers with 1.44 million residents. Designed to be a national, internationalized highland of agricultural innovation, the Agricultural Valley will support bio-breeding, modern planting and breeding, farm and sideline product processing, biotechnologies and products,

务等产业，打造国家种业科技创新中心、现代粮食产业科技创新中心、农业科技成果转移转化中心、农业对外合作交流中心（即“四大中心”），以及农业高新技术产业示范区、智慧（数字）农业示范区（即“两个示范区”）。在功能布局方面，“中原农谷”与国土空间规划相衔接，确定核心区为国际一流农科“芯”城，西区为高新技术转化集成地，东区为粮油产业经济集聚地，南区为食品加工产业示范区。

按照《方案》《规划》，到2025年，“中原农谷”将建成国内一流的种业创新平台，成为带动全省乃至全国农业农村现代化的示范引领区；到2035年，“中原农谷”将建成世界一流的农业科技基础设施集群、科研试验示范基地集群和全球粮食科技创新高地，成为国家区域性农业创新核心力量，深度融入“一带一路”农业科技创新体系，从更高水平上筑牢国家粮食安全根基。

agricultural equipment manufacturing, and modern agricultural services. It will serve as four centers – national seed industry innovation center, modern grain industry innovation center, agro-technological achievements transfer and commercialization center, and international agricultural cooperation and exchange center, and two demonstration zones – agricultural high-tech industrial demonstration zone and smart (digital) agricultural demonstration zone. With its layout matching well with the provincial territorial space plan, the Central Plains Agricultural Valley is divided into four sections – a world-class agricultural science zone, a hub of high-tech commercialization, a center of grain and oil industries, and a demonstration zone for food processing industry.

The place is expected to become a first-class seed innovation platform and a demonstration zone of agricultural and rural modernization in China by 2025. By 2035, it will have in place world-class clusters of agro-technological infrastructure and scientific research and experiment demonstration bases, as well as a global highland of food technology innovation. As a regional powerhouse of agricultural innovation, it will fully engage in the Belt and Road agro-technological innovation system and guarantee national food security at a higher level.

国人厨房

河南位于中原腹地，大部分土地是由黄河冲积而成的肥沃平原，被誉为“中原粮仓”，以占全国6.2%的耕地，生产了中国10%的粮食，粮食总产量连续多年突破6500万吨，不仅养活这个第一农业人口大省，每年还外调出原粮及制成品600多亿斤。同时，河南也是重要的农产品生产加工大省，是中国第一粮食加工大省和第一肉制品大省。

近年来，河南坚持质量兴农、绿色兴农、品牌强农，以保障重要和优质特色农产品供给为目标，以面制品、肉制品、油制品、乳制品、果蔬制品为重点，持续推进食品业转型升级、高质量发展，实现从“中原粮仓”到“国人厨房”的转变。2022年，河南面制品加工能力居全国第一位，粮油加工转化率80%，主食产业化率超过65%；猪、鸡、鹅等畜禽规模化养殖在国内首屈一指，生猪、家禽、肉牛年屠

Kitchen of China

Located in the hinterland of the Central Plains, Henan boasts highly fertile alluvial soils brought by the Yellow River, hence its fame as the "Central Plains breadbasket." With only 6.2 percent of China's arable land, it produces 10 percent of its grain with a total output exceeding 65 million tons for years. While feeding its over 100 million population – the largest for an agricultural province, it also supplies more than 30 billion kilograms of grain and related products to the rest of the country every year. Henan is a major producer and processer of farm products, providing the most processed food products and meat products among all provinces.

In recent years, Henan has promoted green, high-quality agriculture with leading brands and worked to transform and upgrade the food industry to ensure the supply of major, specialty and competitive farm products such as flour, meat, oil, dairy, fruit, and vegetable. This will help turn the "Central Plains breadbasket" into a "kitchen of China."

In 2022, Henan's flour processing capacity ranked first in China, 80 percent of its grain and oil products were processed, and 65 percent of its staple food products were mass-produced. It boasted the largest scale of pig, chicken, goose and other livestock and poultry farming in

宰加工能力分别达8800万头、14亿只、290万头，均位居全国前列；粮食产业总产值突破3000亿元，其中，优势特色农业不断壮大，产值占比57.8%；绿色食品业加快转型升级，规模以上农产品加工企业5109家，年营业收入同比增长6.4%；方便酸辣粉市场份额占全国80%以上。截至2023年3月，河南省农业产业化省级以上重点龙头企业1169家，其中国家级102家、省级1067家。

随着品质的提升，越来越多河南农产品开始漂洋过海，出口到韩国、日本、美国、俄罗斯、西班牙等多个国家和地区。全省形成了一批特色农产品出口生产基地，并实现了区域化布局、标准化生产和规模化经营，国际竞争力不断增强，河南由此实现了由“中原粮仓”到“国人厨房”，再到“世界餐桌”的转变。

the country, and it processed the meat of 88 million pigs, 1.4 billion poultry, and 2.9 million beef cattle, all being the most in China. The total output value of the grain industry surpassed 300 billion yuan. Among that, competitive and specialty agriculture kept growing and accounted for 57.8 percent of the output value. As the green food industry was transforming and upgrading at a faster pace, the number of agro-processing enterprises above the designated scale reached 5,109, whose annual revenue grew 6.4 percent year-on-year. Henan also took over 80 percent of the national market share of instant hot-and-sour rice noodles. As of March 2023, it had 1,169 key enterprises with large scale of agricultural industrialization.

Now, more and more local quality farm products are being exported to the ROK, Japan, the US, Russia, Spain, and other countries and regions. With the development of a number of export-oriented production bases of agricultural specialties with standardized production and large-scale operation, Henan's international competitiveness keeps increasing. The "Central Plains breadbasket" and the "kitchen of China" are now supplying more food on the table of the whole world.

中原城市群

中原城市群是中国北方内陆地区以郑州为中心，依托发达的交通通信网络形成的空间结构紧凑、经济联系紧密的一体化发展城市群体。

2003年8月，中共河南省委、河南省政府印发《河南省全面建设小康社会规划纲要》，提出要建设中原城市群经济隆起带，即以郑州为中心，包括洛阳、开封、新乡、焦作、许昌、平顶山、漯河、济源在内的城市密集区。2016年12月国务院批复的《中原城市群发展规划》，明确中原城市群以河南省郑州市、开封市、洛阳市、平顶山市、新乡市、焦作市、许昌市、漯河市、济源市、鹤壁市、商丘市、周口市和山西省晋城市、安徽省亳州市为核心发展区，联动辐射河南省安阳市、濮阳市、三门峡市、南阳市、信阳市、驻马店市，河北省邯郸市、邢台市，山西省长治市、运城市，安徽省宿州市、阜阳市、淮北市、蚌埠市，山东省聊城市、菏泽市等中原经济区其他城市，要求把中原城市群建设成为经济

Central Plains City Cluster

This refers to the group of cities in China's inland that, with Zhengzhou as the center, are densely located in spatial layout and closely linked in economy and pursue integrated development based on advanced transportation and communication networks.

In an overall plan for building a moderately prosperous society in all respects, issued in August 2003, the provincial authorities set the goal to develop an economic uplift belt in the Zhengzhou-centered area with eight surrounding cities: Jiaozuo, Jiyuan, Kaifeng, Luohe, Luoyang, Pingdingshan, Xinxiang, and Xuchang. The Central Plains City Cluster Development Plan, approved by the State Council in December 2016, made it clear that the Central Plains city cluster would have a core development area to cover Henan's Hebi, Jiaozuo, Jiyuan, Kaifeng, Luohe, Luoyang, Pingdingshan, Shangqiu, Xinxiang, Xuchang, Zhengzhou, and Zhoukou, Shanxi's Jincheng, and Anhui's Bozhou. These cities are expected to drive the development of other cities in the Central Plains economic zone, including Henan's Anyang, Nanyang, Puyang, Sanmenxia, Xinyang, and Zhumadian, Hebei's Handan and Xingtai, Shanxi's Changzhi and Yuncheng, Anhui's Bengbu, Fuyang, Huaibei, and Suzhou, and Shandong's Heze and Liaocheng.

The Central Plains city cluster will be developed

发展新增长极、重要的先进制造业和现代服务业基地、中西部地区创新创业先行区、内陆地区双向开放新高地和绿色生态发展示范区，构建网络化、开放式、一体化的发展新格局。2018年11月，中共中央、国务院发布《关于建立更加有效的区域协调发展新机制的意见》，将中原城市群列为7大城市群之一。

作为中原城市群的核心城市，郑州是区域经济的龙头、发动机、增长极和辐射源，是人口超过1260万、GDP总量超过1.26万亿的特大城市，是内陆地区最大的立体交通枢纽之一，也是全国重要的商品物流和市场交易中心，全国有影响的教育、文化和医疗中心，以汽车、电子信息和高端装备为代表的先进制造业中心，成为国家中心城市之一。

into a new economic growth pole, an important base of advanced manufacturing and modern services, a pioneer zone of innovation and entrepreneurship in central and western China, a highland of two-way opening up in inland China, and a demonstration zone for green, ecological development. This will create a development paradigm that is networked, open, and integrated. The Central Plains city cluster was designated by China's central leadership as one of the seven city clusters in a document, released in November 2018, on creating more effective mechanisms for coordinated regional development.

As the core of the Central Plains city cluster, Zhengzhou is the locomotive, engine, growth pole, and radiation source of the regional economy. A mega-city with a population of 12.6 million and a GDP of 1.26 trillion yuan, it is one of the largest transportation hubs in inland China, an important national center of commodity logistics and transactions, an influential center of education, culture, and medical care, and an advanced manufacturing center represented by automobiles, electronic information, and high-end equipment. Zhengzhou has grown to be a central city in China.

郑州航空港经济综合实验区

郑州航空港经济综合实验区（以下简称郑州航空港区）位于河南省郑州市，是中国首个、目前唯一一个由国务院批准设立的国家级航空港经济发展先行区，是中国内陆首个人民币创新试点和引智试验区之一，也是郑州—卢森堡“空中丝绸之路”先导区。郑州航空港区位于郑州主城区东南约25千米处，地处郑州、开封、许昌黄金三角地带，在国内大循环中具有承东启西、连南贯北的重要地位。全区面积747平方千米，人口近百万人。

郑州航空港区成立于2013年3月，定位为国际航空物流中心、以航空经济为引领的现代产业基地、内陆地区对外开放重要门户、现代航空都市、中原经济区核心增长极，是一个拥有航空、高铁、地铁、城铁、普铁、高速公路与快速路等多种交通方式的立体综合交通枢纽。2021年10月，《黄河流域生态保护和高质量发展规划纲要》明确，要支持郑州航空港经济综合实验区做精做强主导产业，加快郑州国际航空货运枢纽建设。2022年4月，河南省委、省政府以前瞻三十年的眼光，对郑州航空港区进行系统性重塑重构改革，将发展区域拓展为核心区（747平方千米）、联动区（1100平方千米）、协同区（3200平方千米）。

Zhengzhou Airport Economy Zone

The Zhengzhou Airport Economy Zone (Zhengzhou Airport Zone) is China's first and only national pioneer zone of airport economy. It is also the first pilot zone in inland China to do cross-border Renminbi business and introduce overseas talent, and a forerunner zone in building the Zhengzhou-Luxembourg "Air Silk Road."

About 25 kilometers southeast of downtown Zhengzhou, the airport zone, covering 747 square kilometers with a population of nearly one million, is located right in the center of the Zhengzhou-Kaifeng-Xuchang triangle region, commanding an advantageous position of connecting different parts of the country.

Established in March 2013, the zone is designed as an international air logistics center, a modern industrial base led by the aviation economy, an important inland gateway of opening up, a modern aviation city, and a core growth pole in the Central Plains economic zone. It is a comprehensive transportation hub integrating various travel modes, including aviation, high-speed railway, subway, urban rail transit, normal-speed railway, expressway, and fast road. According to the Outline of the Ecological Protection and High-quality Development Plan of the Yellow River Basin, efforts will be made to support the zone in strengthening its leading industries and to speed up the construction of the

目前，郑州航空港区拥有郑州新郑国际机场一类口岸，郑州新郑综合保税区，肉类、药品、活牛、水果、冰鲜水产品、食用水生动物、国际邮件经转口岸等功能性口岸，电子信息、商贸会展两大千亿级产业集群和生物医药、智能装备、半导体、新型显示、新能源、新基建、航空物流、跨境电商八个百亿级产业集群。

2022年，郑州航空港区地区生产总值完成1208.0亿元，十年年均增长14.1%；工业总产值完成5358.4亿元，十年年均增长17.2%；外贸进出口总值完成4707.8亿元，十年年均增长10.3%。

Zhengzhou International Air Cargo Hub.

At present, the Zhengzhou Airport Zone is home to the Xinzheng International Airport, the Xinzheng Comprehensive Bonded Zone, the functional ports for meat, medicine, live cattle, fruits, chilled aquatic products, edible aquatic animals, and international mail transit, two industrial clusters each with a 100-billion-yuan output value (in electronic information; trade, convention, and exhibition), and eight ones each with a 10-billion-yuan output value (in biomedicine, smart devices, semiconductor, new display, new energy, new infrastructure, air logistics, and cross-border e-commerce).

In 2022, the Zhengzhou Airport Zone registered a GDP of 120.8 billion yuan, an industrial output value of 535.84 billion yuan, and a total import and export volume of 470.78 billion yuan, averaging an annual increase of 14 percent, 17 percent, and 10 percent respectively for a decade.

中国（河南）自由贸易试验区

中国（河南）自由贸易试验区由国务院于2016年8月决定设立，2017年4月正式挂牌。中国（河南）自由贸易试验区实施范围119.77平方千米，涵盖三个片区（郑州片区73.17平方千米，开封片区19.94平方千米，洛阳片区26.66平方千米），以及郑州航空港经济综合实验区、中原国际陆港、郑东新区金融集聚区、郑州新郑综合保税区、郑州出口加工区、河南保税物流中心、国家郑州经济技术开发区、国家洛阳经济技术开发区、国家开封经济技术开发区等9个海关特殊监管区域。

自中国（河南）自由贸易试验区成立以来，三个片区围绕产业链条，聚焦企业关注，持续推进政策创新、服务创新，主导产业、特色产业聚集效应逐步显现，一批国际化知名企业在片区布局区域总部、生产基地、软件中心。截至2022年年底，中国（河南）自由贸易试验区累计设立企业12.1万家，是挂牌前的4.4倍；货物进出口年均增长23.8%；以全省万分之七的国土面积，贡献了约16%的新设外资企业数、7%左右的税收和进出口额。

China (Henan) Pilot Free Trade Zone

The China (Henan) Pilot Free Trade Zone was inaugurated in April 2017. Covering 120 square kilometers, the zone has three areas in Zhengzhou, Kaifeng, and Luoyang. It is also home to nine special customs supervision zones – Zhengzhou Airport Economy Zone, Central Plains International Land Port, Zhengdong New Area Financial Hub, Zhengzhou Xinzheng Comprehensive Bonded Zone, Zhengzhou Export-oriented Processing Zone, Henan Bonded Logistics Center, Zhengzhou Economic and Technological Development Zone, Luoyang Economic and Technological Development Zone, and Kaifeng Economic and Technological Development Zone.

Since the China (Henan) Pilot Free Trade Zone was established, a group of world-renowned companies have landed their regional headquarters, production bases, and software centers here, attracted by the innovative local policies and services catering to industrial chains and enterprises' concerns. Leading and distinctive industries are beginning to gather in the zone. By the end of 2022, 121,000 businesses had been established here, and its cargo import and export had grown by 23.8 percent annually on average. The zone was home to 16 percent of the foreign enterprises newly founded in Henan and produced 7 percent of the province's taxation and import and export.

2023年2月，河南省人民政府印发《中国（河南）自由贸易试验区2.0版建设实施方案》，进一步突出制度型开放和创新协同，提升自贸区建设的河南特色优势。

In February 2023, a Version 2.0 plan on the zone's development was released by the provincial government, which aimed to enhance Henan's special strengths through institutional opening up and collaborative innovation.

四路协同

建设内陆开放新高地，是河南发展的美好愿景，也是河南高质量发展的必经之路。地处中原的河南充分发挥区位优势，以“空中丝绸之路”为引领，统筹推进陆上、网上、海上丝绸之路建设，以高水平互联互通和高质量多式联运发展为核心，形成“四路协同”创新集聚发展态势，推动河南实现由内陆腹地向开放高地的历史性转变。

2021年4月，《河南省国民经济和社会发展第十四个五年规划和二〇三五年远景目标纲要》明确“四路协同”水平显著提升的发展目标，部署高水平建设“四条丝绸之路”的战略行动，提出以“空中丝绸之路”为引领，全面推动“四路”联动互促、融合并进，打造具有国际影响力的枢纽经济先行区：提升郑州—卢森堡“空中丝绸之路”品牌优势，打造全球枢纽伙伴网络；以新亚欧大陆桥经济走廊为引领，推动“陆上丝绸之路”扩量提质和运贸一体化发展，打造干支

Four-Route Silk Road

Building an inland highland of opening up is Henan's vision for high-quality development. Leveraging its geographical location in the Central Plains, Henan has devoted due efforts to building the Silk Road on the land, the internet, and the sea while making progress with the Silk Road in the air. With close coordination among these four routes, which feature high-level connectivity and high-quality multi-modal transportation, it strives to achieve a historic transformation from a hinterland to a highland of opening up.

In its 14th Five-year Plan for Economic and Social Development and Long-range Objectives Through the Year 2035, issued in April 2021, Henan set the goal of substantially facilitating the coordination through strategic actions to promote mutually-reinforcing, integrated advances in the four routes.

With the Air Silk Road taking the lead, a pioneering zone of the hub economy with international influence is envisioned: (1) The Zhengzhou-Luxembourg Air Silk Road will be further enhanced to forge a global network of partner hubs. (2) Based on the New Eurasian Land Bridge Economic Corridor, the Land Silk Road will be built with equal emphasis on transportation and trade and with a larger capacity and a higher quality, in order

结合、枢纽集散、贯通欧亚的陆上经济走廊；促进“网上丝绸之路”创新突破，打造国际性跨境电子商务与多元化贸易中心；畅通融入“海上丝绸之路”，深化内陆港设施共建和铁海联运班列线路拓展；创新“四路协同”机制，强化规划统筹、政策互通、设施联通、信息共享、服务联动。

在空中，自2014年6月开通以来，郑州—卢森堡“空中丝绸之路”“双枢纽”合作不断深入，已形成“一点连三洲，一线串欧美”的运营格局，货运航线实现对全球主要经济体全覆盖，货运保障能力位居世界前列。截至2023年8月，郑州机场已开通客货运航线258条，覆盖亚欧美三大洲26个国家和地区200多个城市，出入境货运航班突破1万架次。

在陆上，截至2023年6月底，中欧班列（中豫号）累计开行超8300班，构建了“8个口岸出入境、21条线路直达”的国际物流网络和“1+N”境内外物流枢纽体系，境外业务

to make it a cross-Eurasian economic corridor with both trunk and branch lines and serve as a hub for collection and distribution. (3) Henan will support innovations and breakthroughs to build the Online Silk Road into an international center of cross-border e-commerce and diversified trade. (4) The province will step up the construction of inland port facilities and expand the rail routes for rail-sea intermodal transportation in order to better align itself with the Maritime Silk Road. To better serve these purposes, relevant mechanisms will be improved to facilitate planning coordination, policy communication, infrastructure connectivity, information sharing, and service linkage.

The Air Silk Road: Commencing operation in June 2014, the Zhengzhou-Luxembourg Air Silk Road sees booming cooperation between Zhengzhou and Luxembourg as two key cargo hubs. It now connects Asia, Europe, and America and boasts a world-leading transportation capacity with cargo routes covering all major economies. By August 2023, the Zhengzhou Xinzheng International Airport had opened 258 passenger and cargo routes to more than 200 cities in 26 countries and regions on the three continents and operated more than 10,000 inbound and outbound cargo flights.

The Land Silk Road: By the end of June 2023, the China Railway Express freight trains had made over 8,300 trips between Henan and Europe, building an international logistics network with eight entry and exit ports and

网络辐射40多个国家140多个城市，境内外合作伙伴超过6000家，初步实现“连通境内外，辐射东中西”，成为共建“一带一路”的“钢铁驼队”。

在网上，全球跨境电商大会永久落户郑州，自2017年起已连续举办七届；河南国际贸易“单一窗口”平台处理能力每天3000万单以上，居全国前列。2022年，河南跨境电商进出口交易额首次突破2200亿元，业务辐射196个国家和地区，实现了“买全球、卖全球”的发展目标。

在海上，郑州至天津、连云港、青岛、宁波等港口的7条海铁联运班列已累计开行超过600班；周口相继开通至上海港等6条国内集装箱航线以及至美国洛杉矶长滩港等5条国际航线，实现了“箱通世界、货运全球”。

21 direct routes and a system of domestic and overseas logistics hubs. The overseas business network links more than 140 cities in over 40 countries and more than 6,000 partners at home and abroad. These trains form the "caravans on the rail" that contribute to the Belt and Road cooperation and connect domestic and international markets and the eastern, central and western regions of China.

The Online Silk Road: The Global Cross-border E-commerce Conference, which is permanently based in Zhengzhou, has been held for seven sessions since its inception in 2017. The China (Henan) International Trade Single Window leads the country with a daily handling capacity of more than 30 million deals. In 2022, Henan's import and export volume through cross-border e-commerce exceeded 220 billion yuan for the first time, involving 196 countries and regions and achieving the goal of doing business worldwide.

The Maritime Silk Road: The trains running on the seven rail-sea intermodal routes connecting Zhengzhou with Tianjin, Lianyungang, Qingdao, Ningbo, and other ports have operated 600 shifts, and Zhoukou has opened six domestic container routes to Shanghai and other ports as well as five international routes to ports including the Long Beach in Los Angeles, the US.

建设四大国家文化公园

2021年3月，《中华人民共和国国民经济和社会发展第十四个五年规划和2035年远景目标纲要》提出建设长城、大运河、长征、黄河等国家文化公园。河南是唯一兼具四大国家文化公园建设任务的省份，也是黄河国家文化公园重点建设区。河南将充分发挥这一叠加优势，集中推出一批文化标志物项目，现已谋划300多项国家文化公园相关项目，其中40项重点项目正加紧推进。

河南省黄河国家文化公园建设涉及14个地市，已确立“一核三极、一廊九带”的空间布局（“一核”为郑汴洛大河文明传承创新核心区，“三极”为豫晋陕、豫冀鲁、豫皖苏等3个跨省域联动发展增长极；“一廊”为黄河干流文化旅游廊道，“九带”为伊洛河、古济水—沁河等9条黄河文化旅游带）。

河南省大运河国家文化公园涉及9个地市，主要承担大

Four National Cultural Parks

China's Outline of the 14th Five-year Plan (2021-2025) for Economic and Social Development and Long-range Objectives Through the Year 2035, unveiled in March 2021, proposed to build national cultural parks themed on the Great Wall, the Grand Canal, the Long March, and the Yellow River. This makes Henan the only province to engage in the construction of all of these four national cultural parks and a key area for the construction of the Yellow River National Cultural Park. Siezing this opportunity, Henan has launched a number of signature cultural projects. More than 300 projects have been planned, of which 40 key ones are in full swing.

The Yellow River National Cultural Park involves 14 cities in Henan, featuring "one core, three poles, one corridor, and nine belts." The core refers to the Zhengzhou-Kaifeng-Luoyang core area for the preservation and innovation of the Yellow River civilization; the poles refer to the three cross-provincial regions (Henan-Shanxi-Shaanxi, Henan-Hebei-Shandong, and Henan-Anhui-Jiangsu); the corridor refers to the cultural tourism corridor along the trunk stream of the Yellow River; and the belts refer to the nine Yellow River-themed cultural tourism belts.

The Grand Canal National Cultural Park involves nine cities in Henan. Efforts will be made to protect the

运河河南段（隋唐大运河主干道通济渠、永济渠以及京杭大运河会通河）的建设保护任务，将沿通济渠古都发展轴和永济渠古城发展轴，建设通济渠洛阳片区、郑州片区、开封片区、商丘片区和永济渠焦新片区、安鹤片区、濮阳片区，重点打造25个核心展示园、20条集中展示带，150个特色展示点。

河南省长城国家文化公园涉及7个地市，主要承担春秋战国时期的楚长城、魏长城、赵长城建设保护任务。

河南省长征国家文化公园涉及6个地市，主要承担大别山革命老区和红二十五军长征线路建设保护任务。

“十四五”期间，河南将积极参与建设四大国家文化公园，为全社会提供更多探寻中华文明、触摸华夏历史、感悟黄河文化、体验生态环境的公共开放空间。

Grand Canal's Henan sections – the Tongji Canal and the Yongji Canal of the Sui-Tang Grand Canal and the Huitong River of the Beijing-Hangzhou Grand Canal. A total of 25 core parks, 20 routes, and 150 feature spots will be built along the ancient course of the Tongji Canal in Luoyang, Zhengzhou, Kaifeng, and Shangqiu and along that of the Yongji Canal in the Jiaozuo-Xinxiang, Anyang-Hebi, and Puyang sections.

The Great Wall National Cultural Park involves seven cities in Henan. This will help protect the Great Wall sections built by the State of Chu, State of Wei, and State of Zhao in the Spring and Autumn and the Warring States periods more than 2,000 years ago.

The Long March National Cultural Park involves six cities in Henan. The localities involved will be responsible for the preservation of the old revolutionary area in the Dabie Mountains and the Long March route of the 25th Army of the Red Army.

行走河南·读懂中国

2021年12月，河南省委十一届二次全体（扩大）会议暨省委经济工作会议提出，要塑造“行走河南、读懂中国”品牌。

按照规划部署，河南围绕“行走河南·读懂中国”品牌形象，实施中华文化超级IP工程，积极构建“4+8+N”中华文化超级IP矩阵。其中，4个全球著名文化IP包括以姓氏根亲为代表的老家河南、以天下黄河为代表的大河文明、以华夏古都为代表的中国气象、以太极少林为代表的中国功夫；8个国际知名文化IP包括探寻中国文字的甲骨文文化IP、彰显华夏之光的仰韶文化IP、代表早期中国的二里头文化IP、展示中国气象的隋唐洛阳城文化IP、蕴含中华美学的宋文化IP、感知中国时间的二十四节气文化IP、凝练东方智慧的道家思想文化IP、传达中国意境的唐诗宋词文化IP。此外，河南还将依托古城、古镇、古关、古道等文化遗存，伏

Walking Through Henan, Understanding China

At the economic work conference in December 2021, the provincial authorities decided to launch a campaign on the theme of "Walking Through Henan, Understanding China."

According to the decisions made at the conference, Henan will carry out a mega IP project and create a "4+8+N" super IP matrix, both themed on the Chinese culture. In the matrix, the "4" refers to the "Sweet Home Henan" memory represented by the surname culture, the Yellow River civilization, the culture of the ancient capitals, and the Chinese martial arts represented by *Taijiquan* and the Shaolin *kung fu*. The "8" refers to the oracle-bone inscriptions that help trace the Chinese script, the Yangshao site that verifies the embryo of the Chinese civilization, the Erlitou site that represents China in its early stage, Luoyang of the Sui and the Tang dynasties that showcases the Chinese style, the culture of the Song Dynasty that represents Chinese aesthetics, the 24 solar terms that show how the ancient Chinese marked the passage of time, the indigenous Chinese philosophy of Daoism, and the Tang poems and Song lyrics that express the unique beauty of Chinese literature. The "N" encompasses an array of cultural IPs including cultural heritage sites (e.g. ancient cities, towns, passes and roads), natural views (e.g. Funiu,

牛山、太行山、大别山等自然景观，红旗渠精神、大别山精神、焦裕禄精神、愚公移山精神等民族精神，中国节日、中原美食、中原手作等生活方式，培育若干（N个）全国一流文化IP。

同时，“行走河南·读懂中国”品牌还推出了人类起源、文明起源、国家起源、逐鹿中原、追寻先贤、姓氏寻根、元典思想、治黄史诗、科技发明、四大古都、中国功夫等16条主题文化线路，将历史文化与现代文明融入旅游经济发展，吸引各国游客行走河南，读懂历史巨变中黄河文明的强大凝聚力，感受华夏民族焕然一新的精神风貌，共同向往人类文明进步的美好明天。

Taihang, and Dabie mountains), national ethos (e.g. related to the builders of the Hongqi Canal, the old revolutionary base in the Dabie Mountains, Jiao Yulu, and Yu Gong), and lifestyles (e.g. Chinese festivals, delicious food, and crafts of the Central Plains).

To help people learn more about the province and further understand China, Henan has also launched 16 cultural routes on such themes as the origins of humankind, the Chinese civilization, and China, the rivalry for the control of the Central Plains, the stories about the ancient sages, tracing family roots through surnames, the earliest classical philosophy, the harnessing of the Yellow River, technological inventions, the four ancient capitals, and the Chinese *kung fu*. These will enable the visitors from all countries to experience the powerful cohesion of the Yellow River civilization amid historical changes and the current ethos and outlook of the Chinese nation.

“老家河南”

“老家河南”，朴素地解释为中国人的家乡在河南。河南简称“豫”，位于中国中部，地处黄河中下游，是中华文明发祥地之一，早在50万年前就有人类在这里繁衍生息。

以河南为核心的中原文化博大精深，源远流长。从表层看，中原文化是一种地域文化。从深层看，中原文化是中华民族传统文化的根源和主干，在中华文化发展史上占有突出地位。中国八大古都有4个位于河南，分别为十三朝古都洛阳、八朝古都开封、七朝古都安阳、夏商古都郑州。中华文化中的龙文化、汉字文化、姓氏文化、农耕文化、中医文化、武术文化、大河文化等均起源于河南。河南文化集中展示了中原文化、汉文化的特点，深厚广袤的黄土地滋养了河南人热情纯朴、勤劳善良的品格。

自2009年起，河南省陆续推出系列宣传片《壮美中原，

Sweet Home Henan

Sweet Home Henan, to put it in simple words, means that Henan is the hometown of the Chinese people. Located in central China in the middle and lower reaches of the Yellow River, Henan, usually abbreviated as "Yu," is one of the birthplaces of the Chinese civilization where there were already human activities 500,000 years ago.

Henan is the center of the profound and long-standing Central Plains culture, which is a regional culture on the surface, but is essentially the source and mainstream of the traditional Chinese culture, occupying a prominent position in China's cultural history. Four of the eight major ancient capitals in China are in Henan – Luoyang, capital of 13 dynasties and kingdoms; Kaifeng, capital of 8 ruling courts; Anyang, capital of 7 kingdoms and dynasties; and Zhengzhou, capital of the Xia and the Shang dynasties. Many key and popular concepts in the Chinese culture, such as the totem of the dragon, Chinese characters, surnames, farming culture, TCM, martial arts, and the Yellow River civilization, all originated in Henan. The province is the embodiment of the Central Plains culture and the Han culture, and its fertile land has nurtured its kind, honest and hard-working people.

Since 2009, Henan has launched a series of promotional videos, such as "Sweet Home Henan: the

老家河南》《记忆中原，老家河南》《豫见中国，老家河南》，在塑造传播河南形象的同时，明确提出了“老家河南”的概念，建构了“老家河南”这一文化品牌。作为中原文化核心的河南，是贯通古今的重要节点，在积极融入“一带一路”、开展对外交流中，展现着中华之源、源远流长、交流互鉴、创新创造、融合发展的“老家河南”，呈现古老与时尚完美交融的出彩形象，不断吸引海外人士游河南、观中国。

Magnificent Central Plains," "Sweet Home Henan: the Central Plains in History," and "Meet China in Sweet Home Henan." In presenting its image, the province has cultivated the cultural brand of "Sweet Home Henan," which is defined by such keywords as the origin of the Chinese nation, long history, exchanges and mutual learning, innovation and creativity, and integrated development. Being the core of the Central Plains culture and a pivot in Chinese history, Henan is actively merging into the Belt and Road cooperation and engaging in international exchanges, appealing to more overseas visitors with a brilliant combination of antiquity and modernity.

图书在版编目（CIP）数据

中国关键词 . 出彩河南篇 : 汉英对照 / 中国外文出版发行事业局等著 ; 向娜译 . -- 北京 : 新世界出版社 , 2024.6

ISBN 978-7-5104-7774-4

Ⅰ . ①中… Ⅱ . ①中… ②向… Ⅲ . ①中国特色社会主义－社会主义建设模式－研究－汉、英②社会主义建设成就－河南－汉、英 Ⅳ . ① D616 ② D619.61

中国国家版本馆 CIP 数据核字 (2023) 第 235220 号

中国关键词：出彩河南篇（汉英对照）

作　　者：中国外文出版发行事业局　当代中国与世界研究院
　　　　　中国翻译研究院　中共河南省委外事工作委员会办公室
翻　　译：向　娜
审　　定：韩清月　宋金莹
改　　稿：Salil Bissessur [英]
核　　稿：王晓宇
项目统筹：申　阳
项目执行：华光灿　陈晓星
责任编辑：赵如意
装帧设计：魏芳芳　贺玉婷
责任校对：宣　慧　张杰楠
责任印制：王宝根
出　　版：新世界出版社
网　　址：http://www.nwp.com.cn
社　　址：北京西城区百万庄大街 24 号（100037）
发 行 部：(010)6899 5968（电话）(010)6899 0635（电话）
总 编 室：(010)6899 5424（电话）(010)6832 6679（传真）
版 权 部：+8610 6899 6306（电话）nwpcd@sina.com（电邮）
印　　刷：天津中印联印务有限公司
经　　销：新华书店
开　　本：880mm×1230mm　1/32　　尺　　寸：120mm×200mm
字　　数：150 千字　　印　　张：8
版　　次：2024 年 6 月第 1 版　　2024 年 6 月第 1 次印刷
书　　号：ISBN 978-7-5104-7774-4
定　　价：58.00 元